From the author of the USA Today Best Seller
"World's Best Kept Beauty Secrets"

Insider Beauty

Secrets of the Fit & Fabulous

by
Diane Irons

Insider Beauty
Secrets of the Fit & Fabulous

Diane Irons
International Image Inc.
Wakefield, MA

Other Books by Diane Irons

World's Best Kept Beauty Secrets
Age Defying Beauty Secrets
911 Beauty Secrets
World's Best Kept Diet Secrets
Bargain Beauty Secrets
Beauty Boot Camp
Teen Beauty Secrets
Secret Beauty
Real Secrets of Beauty

This publication is designed to provide accurate and authoritative information in regard to the subject matter covered. It is sold with the understanding that the publisher is not involved or engaged in rendering legal, accounting, or other professional service. If legal advice or other expert assistance is required, the services of a competent person should be sought. ------*From a Declaration of Principles Jointly Adopted by a Committee of the American Bar Association and a Committee of Publishers and Associations.*

All brand names and product names used in this book are trademarks, registered trademarks, or trade names of their respective holders. International Image Inc. is not associated with any product or vendor in this book.
This book is not intended as a substitute for medical advice or diagnosis. The intent of this book is to provide accurate general information in regard to the subject matter covered. If medical advice or other expert help is needed, the services of an appropriate medical professional should be sought.

Published by International Image Inc.
(781)245-9593
www.dianeirons.com
Library of Congress Cataloging-in-Publication Data
Irons, Diane Insider Beauty⊏Secrets of the Fit and Fabulous/Diane Irons
p.cm.Includes bibliographical references and index
ISBN
    1. Beauty, Personal

In Memory of

Keith Andrew Irons

1979-1986

Acknowledgements

I wish to thank my wonderful family for all their love and support through the best and most challenging of times.

To my husband David, you are everything good in my life and my best friend.

To my son Kirk, I am so very proud of the exceptional man that you have become. I'm honored to be your mom.

Table of Contents

Introduction

What is an Insider?

I consider an insider someone who has the ability to construct beauty, or the creativity to replicate it.

Some talented hair stylists are insiders. Those who are take their skills beyond their training and intuit the best way to serve their clients beyond the cookie cutter or traditional.

Makeup artists become insiders when they learn to work with flaws and non traditional beauty while not overlooking the individuality of their subject.

Designers and stylists who are the backbone of the clothes we admire on the runway and our favorite TV shows are insiders. They possess a quick response knack for putting together a spectacular look, regardless of budget or time constraints.

Fitness trainers are the most intimate of insiders, seeing their clients from a vulnerable perspective in order to get a camera ready result.
Women who look fantastic in their own unique way may have been born insiders or learned along the way. They are the true insiders.

Why Do We Want Their Secrets?

Why wouldn't we? If we could learn how to handle all our beauty and body dilemmas in a quicker, less expensive, easier way with fabulous results wouldn't we run for the information?

My Life on the Inside

From my earliest memories I have been fascinated with beauty and style. I would play "dress up" with my mother and aunt's clothing and shoes, adapt and cut and style my dolls' hair and wardrobe until they looked just like I imagined. The experimentation didn't stop with my dolls. My sisters and friends would be set upon for my experimental makeovers, many times under protest, other times by sources of pure bribery.

Introduction

Some young girls go kicking and screaming to allocution lessons and charm school. I, on the other hand, begged my parents to attend as many classes as possible.
When I was an awkward but curious 14, the hair company Breck came to town looking for fresh faces.

All the girls in my school were called in for a walk through. I was chosen, and that's how the modeling started. Although modeling was fun, what was more interesting to me was what was going on behind the scenes. I loved the transformations and the creativity inside the world of beauty and fashion.

After college, my radio, TV, and newspaper journalism career emerged to give me access to countless celebrities. When women get together, famous or not, they love to talk about girly stuff. It was always a light hearted break, and they loved to gossip and share. I believe that the principal reason I was able to get all this information from them is because I was able to go beyond their product endorsement and get them to open up about their everyday regimes. Plus, it's so much less intimidating to talk about skin care and diet secrets than their love lives.

I used all this experience to train other up and coming models, and went on to open my own agency. I've continued to pass everything I've ever learned to my clients, models, and now to you. While I share the insider tips I've learned, I continued to get new ideas and techniques. We are all students as well as teachers in every aspect of our lives.

Chapter 1
Insider Basics

Have you often wondered just how those gorgeous creatures that grace the runways and the Red Carpets look that way? Do they really spend all day working out? Are they surrounded by extra arms that at their disposal? There are secrets that those on the Inside just aren't willing to share. Why?

There are lots of reasons, but much of the time it's because the secret they are keeping is not related to a product endorsement that they are under contract to or are hoping to get. The entire beauty industry is about money, endorsements, and exclusivity of information. They all want you to know that all they do is drink lots of water! Oh sure, and we really believe them. You don't have to guess that I'm not very popular sharing these secrets from behind the scenes. There's a reason I feel the need to share. All women have the right to look and feel their very best. It creates a state of mind that colors the rest of your world. When you feel together, everything is just a bit easier. Things around you just seem to fall into place.

We can all benefit from new ideas. I hope that you use this book whenever you feel you need a tune up, or need to form a new state of mind. Please consider this book advice not only from me, but personalized advice from the many pros that have created these techniques and passed them on to the originators of the world's most noted looks.

You'll find the celebrity looks you love, and learn how to create them for your own unique style. You'll learn to become an expert at picking just the right colors for your face and body. You'll find out how to determine the exact shade and type of foundation that best matches your skin tone. You'll learn how to take care of your hair in between salon visits. You'll discover tools of the trade and how to use them.
You'll enjoy creating your best new look!

Insider Rules
1. They know that to look and feel their best is a work in progress.
2. They concentrate on what they can do, not what is unattainable.
3. They know how to sift through all the misinformation
4. They all started in the same place.

5. They learn quickly by practicing.
6. They maintain what they've learned.
7. What they can't fix they cover up or divert attention from.
8. They keep changing and reinventing their looks.
9. They create their image to fit their lifestyle.

Insiders Have Attitude

Insiders don't care if their beauty is unconventional. They're proud that they're like no one else. They don't follow rules. They create them. These beauties revel in being noticed, if you like what they're doing or not.

If their looks are not the norm, they work with what they have, and even accentuate the unusual. They revel in standing out. They are comfortable with their looks, whether created or genetic.

Insiders Make Time

Whether it's setting the alarm clock 30 minutes earlier than they need to, or setting out a block of time for themselves on a consistent basis they take it from where they can. It might be from a TV show, internet surfing, or shopping.

Insiders Simplify

They keep only what really works for them and makes them look and feel fabulous, tossing anything that keeps them from feeling or looking good about themselves or their lives. They know that what they look like on the outside affects their inner being.

Insider beauties know who they are and who they will never be. They stay in the niche that works for them. The tall elegant beauty doesn't try to become cute and bubbly. Gwyneth Paltrow doesn't try to emulate Shakira because it will never work.

What Insiders Trust

1. They trust a compliment when they get one. They don't believe that it is being given just because someone was trying to be polite.
2. They trust their mirrors. They accept what they see.

Insiders Are Ageless

Beyond plastic surgery, there is an ageless quality about insider beauties that makes age irrelevant. They don't feel that they are confined by their chronological age. Their hair is in the style that is most flattering, not particularly age appropriate. Their makeup is done to accent their features, not because someone told them that only subdued colors were appropriate for women of a certain age.

Insiders Rely on Their Inner Clock

They don't rely on the time of day to eat. They intuit their hunger. They let their body tell them when it needs to rest. Relying on their inner signals never fails them. I have found insider beauties to be highly intuitive with their bodies.

They Set Goals

Insiders maintain goals, but always insure that their goals are realistic. This keeps them from becoming overwhelmed, and to be able to attain everything they wish to achieve. You can do the same by taking small steps to your ultimate look.

They Have a Standby Plan

Looking great takes some planning ahead. Insider beauties always have a few classic pieces on hand that will take them anywhere at a moment's notice. They have a makeup bag of essentials that they can apply in seconds. Heaven forbid the dog gets loose or we run out milk.
They have a fabulous coat that they can wear over anything.

They Strut Their Stuff

It's not only the techniques, the clothes, or the makeup that is most evident in great beauties. It's the very way they walk, talk, and stand. It's an inner pride knowing that they have done all that they could that makes them look so much better.

Only the Beauty Stands Out

The clothing, the hair, or the makeup is not what you notice about an insider beauty. Those things are just a support team to the beauty who's using them. And she knows how to use these things so that they remain in the background, accenting rather than overcoming the total picture. So if you see an insider beauty what you see is the beauty, you don't concentrate on the lipstick or blush.

Insiders Consider Themselves a Canvas

Although they work with what they were given by nature, insider beauties become a blank slate when working on their appearance. Just because they are a "cool" color tone doesn't mean that they won't wear red or purple if those are the colors they love. Perhaps they were born blonde, but that doesn't mean they won't live for a while as a redhead (that is until something they like better comes around).

They Have It Their Way

Insiders dictate fashion; they will never blindly follow it. If their asset is great legs, pity the foolish and pompous fashion designer who tells them that short skirts are out. If their hair is big and beautiful and yet the style of the day is straight ironed tresses shown close to the head it's just too bad.

No False Modesty Here

When it's all together and working like it should, those lovely insiders will take all the credit. They're proud of their looks and the work it took to get to that place, and they accept all compliments.

Insiders are Flexible

They can go with the flow and come out looking not only unscathed, but just fine, thank you.

Insiders Maintain a Sense of Humor

They have the ability to respect their looks, but not to take them too seriously. They will try something new, and if it doesn't work, they'll just shrug it off, and go on to something else.

"I have a very, very, very good relationship with myself."
Diane von Furstenberg

Insiders Visualize

When insiders want to change their looks they visualize specific changes that they want to make. Whether they want clearer skin, firmer thighs, or shinier hair, they think ahead to how their look will end up.

Insiders Listen

The most reliable beauty guru the insider has is her own inner voice. Once you tune in to yours it won't let you down. That inner voice can reason out why we over ate, why we're feeling stressed, or nudge us to pluck our eyebrows.

Insiders are Fearless

They go for the beauty dares. They try that odd combination or unusual hair style.
If absolutely no one on this planet has worn it, it doesn't bother them a bit, actually it's so much the better.
Insiders are the trend makers. If they wear it one day, then you can bet that it becomes the sought after "look" the next day.
And this doesn't only apply to big names. An insider trend setter can be as close as the classroom, board meeting, or office.

Insiders Consider Vanity a Virtue

Their self care is a source of pride and great achievement for them. It allows the insider beauty to learn about style and glamour while learning about themselves.

We are spiritual, intellectual, emotional, and physical beings. We cannot ignore our physicality. By caring for our physical selves we are experiencing all the aspects of who we really are.

Chapter 2
Insider Skin

The Secret to a Smooth and Flawless Complexion

It's what we all seek, and the basis of a healthy glowing appearance.
Here's what you need to know to have that much sought after insider's complexion.

Great Skin Starts from the Inside

Water is the number one route to great skin. Don't just drink it when you're thirsty, because if you wait until then your skin is already parched. Carry it with you wherever you go. It will keep your skin bright and glowing, flushing out toxins, and deeply hydrating and plumping skin.

Insider Tip

Insider beauties keep water bottles frozen, so they can grab them and go and stay hydrated throughout the day. The water will slowly defrost.

Keep It Cold

Drinking ice cold water is a key insider beauty secret. Your body will heat itself up in order to absorb the water, burning up to 35 calories with each eight ounce bottle consumed. Studies at the University of Switzerland have heavily documented this all important difference.

Cleanse Ever So Gently

The biggest mistake those on the outside of the beauty circle make is over cleansing. Insiders know that there is no need to do anything but rinse even the oiliest face in the morning. If you need to scrub something in the morning, scour your sink. You have done nothing all night but lay on that pillow. A few oils may have accumulated, but your face has not become dirty. Unless you are in need of a cleaner pillow case there is no way that your face is in need of soap in the morning.

If you absolutely must use something more than water, take a dime sized amount of powdered milk and add it to enough water to create a soft paste. This mixture will gently cleanse and exfoliate at the same time. I hope you start treating your face less harshly. You're only irritating your skin unnecessarily.

Exfoliating Techniques

You really only need to exfoliate your face two or three times a week. Use gentle circular strokes and work the exfoliant into the crevices of your skin. There are many exfoliants on the market today. Avoid rough or coarse particles when selecting one. Certain brands can tear delicate skin fibers.

An at home microdermabrasion kit is a cost effective major exfoliating process, and will greatly improve skin's tone and texture. It's usually done once a week and is a two step process. Look for kits that feature self heating.

Insider Toning Secrets

Insiders know that most toners contain alcohol, too drying for sensitive facial skin. Toners should only be applied where oils collect. Press toner saturated on a cotton ball into the crease of the nose, on the forehead, and chin area. It's not necessary to tone the entire face unless there is makeup residue.

Toner Options

There is one toner used most often behind the scenes. It's good old fashioned witch hazel, and it can usually be purchased at drugstores for less than two dollars. It will last forever!

For very oily skin or extremely clogged pores use hydrogen peroxide mixed with an equal amount of warm water. Apply it with a cotton ball and rinse thoroughly after blotting at the most severe areas.

Be Careful with Lip Balm

The same ingredients that make balms feel like they're working (such as menthol and camphor) are actually pulling moisture from lips. This leads to more cracking and the need for more lip balm.

Solution: Switch to a moisturizing lipstick or a balm made primarily from Aloe, which actually heals the lips.

Skin Issues

Windburn

Windburn is caused by cold temperatures and brisk winds, taking away natural moisturizing oils from the top layer of skin. The result is chapped, red, and often swollen skin. Chamomile tea, or if you can find it at your health food store, German chamomile essential oil, restores the skin when used two to three times a day.

Irritated Skin

Soothe irritated skin with an equal mixture of almond oil and warm water.
Massage in and let set a minute.
Lightly rub off with a damp washcloth.

Rosacea

This is a condition that resembles a breakout or flushed cheeks. To treat and disguise the redness, first apply undiluted dandruff shampoo to the area for about 3 to 5 minutes.
Then add a small amount of green eye shadow into concealer or foundation, and with a sponge apply it to the redness. Green and red are complementary shades on the color wheel and cancel each other out.

Licorice root is an effective homeopathic remedy. Use it overnight, applied to the skin and covered with a small gauze pad.

Prevent a Wine Flush

Sip a cup of black tea before drinking alcohol. It contains quercetin, which decreases the number of mast cells (inflammatory agents) from being released. Doing this will help to prevent those highly colored cheeks that appear after a glass or two of wine or alcohol.

Minimize Large Pores

To temporarily shrink the appearance of large, open pores, apply lemon juice mixed with an equal amount of water.
A more advanced solution is to treat the area with Retinol. Its properties help build collagen and elastin and smoothes out skin.

Smooth Out Pores

In a pinch, apply mattifying lotion over clean skin. Let it set for about 20 to 30 seconds and then apply foundation over it. A mattifying lotion contains silicone that will fill in pores giving a smooth appearance to the skin.

Skin Aids

Sleep Your Way to Better Skin

A lack of sleep leads to stress which can alter the body's chemistry by causing the body's production of cortisol to rise. This hormone can cause the body to experience increased inflammatory damage. Although sleep requirements vary, the recommended sleep cycle for optimum health is from seven to nine hours.

Insiders rely on lavender sachets to help them get a solid night's sleep. Purchase them in sachet form or make your own. Lavender is available at any health food store or natural supermarket. Place 2 to 3 tablespoons in a jewelry pouch.

Fight Skin Inflammation with Supplements

Vitamins C and E as well as Alpha Lipoic acid are all effective in fighting inflammatory damage brought on by free radicals in the body.

Also consider adding fish oil supplements to your daily diet. Important to your overall health, fish oil contains omega-3 fatty acids which are highly effective in fighting inflammation

Diet

Whole grains, fruits and vegetables in deep colors fight inflammation which can cause skin irritation and wrinkling of the skin.
Olive oil, nuts, and cold water fish contain anti-inflammatory properties.
Flaxseed is favored by beauties who have great skin. They use it as a garnish on foods and take it as a supplement.
Spices that help to fight inflammation include ginger and turmeric.

Choosing Skin Care Products

1. The fewer active ingredients in a skin product, the less opportunity for your skin to be thrown off balance.
2. The less preservatives contained in a product will mean that there is less risk of irritation. Check expiration dates on all labels. The longer the date of expiration generally means that that there are more preservatives to stabilize the product.

Dull Flaky Skin

Over the Counter

Look for an exfoliant containing micro beads of vitamin C.
Check to see if the product contains a face peeling acid.

Home Remedy

Mix a quarter cup orange juice with 1 teaspoon of water.
Apply evenly all over the face, and allow to set for a minute or two.
Rinse with tepid water.
The vitamin C in orange juice will help repair skin cells and naturally exfoliate flakes and dryness.

Skin Discoloration

Over the Counter Solution

Look for a hydroquinone product. It's usually called "Out Spot" or "Fading Cream".
It should contain 2% hydroquinone, the highest percentage allowed to be sold without prescription. Anything less will not be effective or worth your effort.

Laser Therapy

If you have very deep skin discoloration, you may consider spending the extra money and time to have the deepest spots zapped.

Home Remedy

With a soft toothbrush rub a mixture of baking soda mixed with just enough fresh lemon juice to create a soft paste into the skin. Allow it to set for one minute. Rinse off with warm water.

Erase Fine Lines

Home Remedy

Caffeine is the hot ingredient in the priciest of skin care. Save money and get a more powerful product by taking a minute or two to reach for your own cooled java.

Apply the cooled coffee (the stronger the better) to the lines. Caffeine firms skin and plumps wrinkles.

Coffee also strengthens skin against free radicals, and even reduces skin cancer risk. It's an insider skin must do.

Treat Unsightly Acne

Over the Counter

Look for Salicylic Acid treatments. These will unclog pores and clean them out.

Home Remedies

Rub tomato pulp all over your face. Leave it on for about 20 minutes. Rinse thoroughly.

Hold an ice cube on the pimple to bring down the swelling.
Apply tea tree oil with a cotton swab and hold for 60 seconds. Tea tree oil contains anti-viral properties that zap blemish causing bacteria on contact.

Conceal the redness with an eye redness remover. Add green eye shadow to your concealer or foundation to neutralize the redness.
Blend in and then apply foundation.

The Aspirin Mask

Dissolve 3 aspirin in a quarter cup of hot water.
Allow it to cool, and then dip a cotton ball into the mixture.
Apply all over face and allow to set for about ten minutes.
Rinse thoroughly.

The salicylic acid in the aspirin will brighten and even out skin tone while treating acne.

The Vodka Glow

Mix a quarter cup of vodka with the juice of a fresh lemon.
Dab it on the face neck, and chest area.
Don't rinse.
Allow the air to evaporate it.
You will glow girl!

Chapter 3
Making Up

The Miracle of Makeup

Makeup is the perfect accessory! Using it is not only an expression of style and taste, it's a tool to looking and feeling better while boosting confidence. How you apply your makeup will signify the difference between looking like a styling diva or a performing mime. Remember, the reason you wear makeup is to look better, not to look like you're wearing great makeup. Practice and updating will keep you in the current style and looking fabulous!

You Need the Right Tools

Makeup artists are very aware that all the right makeup in the world just won't get the effect it's supposed to without the right brushes. Cosmetic brushes can be exorbitantly expensive. But you can purchase high quality brushes at alternatives to cosmetic counters at reasonable pricing.

1. Art supply stores have wonderful brushes at very low prices.
2. Some mass merchandise stores have arts & crafts departments that feature art quality brushes at extra discounted pricing. Look for packaged bundles for extra savings.

Foundation Application

First and foremost, make sure your skin is well moisturized so that the foundation will go on more smoothly.
Less is more when it comes to foundation. You don't want to look like you're wearing a mask. Dot foundation on with a brush or smudge it with your fingers only where you need it. Blend, blend, blend.

Foundation Check Up

Examine your work next to a window.
Look for signs of creases, streaks or obvious color lines.

Create a Glowing Finish

After applying your foundation, warm a dab of moisturizer in the palms of your hands. Gently press on cheeks and forehead for a natural glow. This technique provides just "enough" shine .

What Kind of Foundation Is Right for You?
Read the description on the bottle. Look for hints like "light skin" or "golden tones".
Take your choice to the window in the store. Hold it to your jaw line.
If you can't decide between foundation shades, go with the darker shade. An application of powder will make the color a bit lighter.

Find Your Perfect Formula
Shiny or oily skin types should choose oil free or cream to powder formulas.
Combination skin find stick foundations work best.
Dry skin benefits from cream based foundations.

Insiders Tip
Look for silicone in the new foundation formulas. It makes the foundation evaporate quickly; leaving the color locked onto your skin, yet feels comfortable.

Get Your Makeup to Stay Put!

Mascara
Here's how to keep mascara from running and getting it to stay on throughout the day. Apply one coat, then dip a cotton swab into loose powder and quickly but gently apply it to the very tips of your wet lashes. Allow it to dry for 30 seconds. Follow with a second coat of mascara.

Wand Trick
Bend the mascara wand at a right angle to apply a perfect coat, and to insure a steady hand. Always crimp your lashes first with a curler to make them more uniform so that the mascara will go on less clumpy.

Mix Mascaras
Apply one coat of lash lengthening mascara and then one coat of waterproof mascara.
The combination of the two mascaras will add drama and extra volume.

Eye Shadow

Apply foundation over the entire eye lid. Cover over with powder.

Mix cream eye shadow with a small amount of color matching powdered shadow.

Apply all over lid by patting, not sweeping strokes.

Add a small amount of baby oil or petroleum jelly to powdered shadow to create an extra vibrant look.

Eyebrow Tamer

For unruly brows, makeup artists rely on moustache wax.

Insider tip

When eye shadow falls onto face, remove it with a piece of Scotch tape.

Concealer

Choose a concealer that exactly matches your skin tone.

Always apply it with your finger so that the warmth of your finger will allow the concealer to blend thoroughly and smoothly.

Concealer should go on after you've applied foundation. Then you can see exactly where you need to cover up.

Apply concealer using a regular mirror, not a magnifying mirror. Otherwise you might over apply.

Powder

Setting your makeup with powder is an effective way to make your skin look soft and finished as well as prevent shine and keep your makeup looking fresh.

Insiders prefer loose powder over pressed powder because there is less chance of caking and streaking.

1. Before applying powder make sure that the foundation is well blended. Blot with a tissue, concentrating on forehead, chin, and nose.
2. Pick up a small amount of powder with a puff and then press the powder firmly on the

face, one area at a time.

3. Using a soft thick powder brush, remove any excess. Use downward strokes to prevent the powder from remaining on facial hair.
4. Brush off any powder from eyebrows and lashes with a brow brush.

Use shimmer powder in only one or two areas. Most flattering to the face is to place it on the top of the cheekbones and along the bridge of your nose. Get a sexy pout by placing a dab at the center of your bottom lip.

Insiders Tip
Always tap puff or brush on a hard surface to remove excess before applying to face.

Create the Insider Smoky Eye

Here's an easy way to replicate the glamorous smoky eye appeal of the runways.

1. Apply a cream concealer to your lids
2. Lightly sweep a cream colored powder shadow across your brow bone.
3. Sweep a charcoal or dark brown shadow from your lash line to your crease.
4. Follow with a dark matte shadow in the same color family, drawing a thin line across and into the top and bottom lash lines.
5. Finish with black or dark brown eyeliner on the inner rim of your bottom lashes.
6. Curl lashes and apply several coats of mascara.

Insider Tip
If you have a hard time getting a perfect look with your liner, apply it in dots and then slightly smudge it.

Create Model Cheekbones
Brush powder blush along the apples of your cheeks and up toward your hairline.
Finish with a bit of highlighter on the high points of your cheeks to create the illusion of higher cheekbones.

Insider Tip

To avoid "striping" your blush, make an "x" across the apple of your cheek and then blend. It will look more natural.

The Perfect Blush Color

Match your blush to the skin inside your lower lip.
Lighten up blush by separating a facial tissue, and then pressing it into blushed area.
This will take away any excess, and blend blush with the rest of the makeup application.

Make Blush Last Longer

Apply cream blush to your cheeks and then dust the area lightly with a translucent powder.
This sets the blush in place without changing its color.

Get Twice the Size Eyes

Line the rim of your lower lids with a creamy white eye pencil.

Curl and mascara your lash. Bend your mascara wand at a 90 degree angle. It will give you more control and you'll be able to push the wand through each of your lashes instead of from the side.

Make your eyes look bigger by extending your eye shadow just above your eyelid crease, arching back and forth on the crease with a darker shadow.

Fake an Instant Nose Job!

Apply foundation one shade lighter than your regular shade down the center of the nose to the tip.
Dab a touch of bronzer on the nostrils and tip.
In an instant you have created the illusion of a thin and chiseled nose.

Get Lip Color to Last

Line the edges of your mouth and fill in your lips with a pencil that matches your natural lip color. Then apply your lip shade with a brush to deliver an even amount of product. This will also prevent feathering.

Get Fuller Looking Lips

Use an eye shadow brush and trace the lip line with a concealer that is one shade darker than your regular skin tone. This will create an ever so slight shadow that gives the illusion of a fuller mouth.

Go Natural

Creating a natural look takes the ability to make your look as lovely as possible with as little makeup as necessary.

1. Use a light foundation or mix foundation with moisturizer.
2. Apply concealer only where needed.
3. Use a soft pink blush.
4. Skip eye shadow or apply a sheer bronze tone.
5. One coat of mascara is all you need. Concentrate the wand at the outside of the eye.
6. Use a lip gloss or mix lip balm with your lipstick.

Pick the Perfect Red Lipstick

Consider Skin Tone

Pink skin tones are best suited with plum based shades.
Yellow shading look best in warmer brown based reds.
Dark skin tones are complemented with pinkish reds.

Consider Lip Size

Smaller lips should wear lip gloss or glaze.
Larger lips look best in matte lipsticks

Anti Aging Makeup

The first issue of making up an older face is that of evening out skin tone. A young face is perfectly even in tone with light reflection.

Lips

Stay away from bright red lips after the age of 40.
Red glaze or a softer red is more flattering.

Cheeks

Always apply blush in a full smile.

Eyes

Always apply a bright eye color in the center or "ball" of the eye.

Concealer

An effective concealer that will match perfectly with your foundation is located right inside the lid of your foundation. It's slightly drier and will provide a thicker coating.

Contouring

Bronzer and blush are not tools for contouring. Insiders use powder a shade darker than the regular face shade. It's subtle and effective.

Make Lips Look Larger

Swipe concealer outside the lips after applying lipstick. The concealer will provide definition to the lips and also keep them from bleeding.

Makeup Can Transform

Anyone who's seen those "candid" pictures of celebrities without makeup wonders how that complete transformation can be achieved. Without makeup they look well, "like us", and yet on the Red Carpet and Screen flawless.

Curling Cue

Curl your lashes and keep them curled longer by heating your lash curler with your hair dryer for just a few seconds. Test to make sure it's not hot, just warm.

Find Your Perfect Shade

Foundation

Match the skin to the area where your jaw line meets your face. The color should fade into the skin with no evident line or color.

Blush

Choose the shade that is closest to your natural flush after you've had a workout.
I bet you anything that it's not going to be orange or brown.

Bronzer

Using bronzer all over can make skin look flat or even "dirty". Finish off bronzer with a pop of pink or peach blush over the apples of your cheeks.

Lipstick

When picking a lip color, test it on your fingertip and not your hand as most women do. Your fingertip has the same blue tones as your lips.

Eye Shadow

The key is to complement to your eye color. The secret to doing this without spending a fortune on mistakes is to take crayons and draw lines of as many colors as you need to find the best choices. If you can't find exactly what you're looking for, combine two or three colors until you find just what you need.

Secrets from Makeup Artists

To create a dewy and soft looking complexion slightly moisten fingers when applying foundation.

If you use a sponge, first wet it, and then thoroughly wring it out before dipping it into the foundation.

Cover Up Redness

Choose foundation with yellow undertones to even out blotchy skin and redness. Don't worry, it won't look yellow once applied.

Lighting

Avoid overhead lighting when applying makeup. It shows every flaw and encourages product over application.

Taupe Eye Shadow

Make up artists always keep taupe eye shadow by their side when working on clients.

It works to fill in brows, creating a soft, natural appearance.

Wet it and it becomes a long lasting, natural liner.

Insider Trick

Cleanse tired skin with menthol. Rub it briskly in a circular motion. Go to the men's aisle to find mentholated cleansers at a reasonable price.

Test first on your wrist for sensitivity.

Tackle Your Makeup Mess

You won't have to "fish" around for your makeup if you store it in a tackle box from the hardware store. That's exactly what smart models and most makeup artists use to lug around their supplies.

Black is not Black

Used in the traditional way, black eyeliner gives off a harsh look. After application, lightly smudge the line to soften. Insiders use a fine brush dipped into a dark brown eye shadow to blend without messing up the line. This method also insures that the result will not look too messy.

Insider Tip

After applying lipstick trace over the bow of your lip with a skin toned highlighter. Blend slightly outward.
This gives the lip a "pouty" look.

Eye Lights

Add gold glitter to cream eye liner to light up your eyes and make them sparkle!

Chapter 4
Model Secrets

Inside the Secrets of Modeling

Models are privy to insider tips on a daily basis. If they are smart, they use these tips to advance their careers.

What they learn behind the runways can also lengthen their time on the runway. Any model that is knowledgeable and cooperative is seen as an asset to the industry.

Model Beauty

Create the Model Brow

You can create those perfectly arched brows of the top super models. First you need the right tools:

Cuticle Scissors

Tweezers

Clear Mascara

White Eye Pencil

Eyebrow Pencil close to your eyebrow color

1. Use the white pencil to outline the exact shape you want.
2. Use the clear mascara and brush your brows up.
3. Allow the mascara to dry on your brows so the hair stands up.
4. Using the cuticle scissors, carefully trim any long hairs above the upper brow line.
5. Tweeze the hairs, one at a time, outside the line, in the direction it grows.
6. Brush brows into place.

Model Eye Tricks

Purchase a creamy black pencil made with beeswax.

Using a fat headed brush, and coat it with color.

Use short feathery strokes, and brush in between lashes and along the entire length of the tops of your lashes.

Follow with two coats of mascara.

Mascara Application

Hold the mascara wand in a vertical position while applying. It provides more volume to the lash.

Apply to the tip of the lashes, concentrating on the outer corners.

Insider Tip

Don't brush on shadow; instead pat the shadow on the lid for optimum color effect, and to allow the shadow to be properly deposited.

Create Model Cheekbones

Not all models have defined cheekbones. Creating them is something that makeup artists and now you can do in just seconds.

With a very soft brush, combine different shades of blush so there's a mixture of light and dark colors. Then from just below the apples in the center of the cheek, swirl the blush toward the temples

Create the Model "Winged" Eye

To get a perfect winged line on a model's eye, we hold a business card under the lower lash and angle it up toward the brow. Use an eye liner brush dipped in dark brown or charcoal powder, then dust lightly along the card's edge. After removing the card, a perfectly straight line will appear. It will not give off that harsh "Cleopatra" line because it is softened by the shadow.

Lipstick Trick for Whiter Teeth

To make teeth look absolutely dazzling just use your lipstick. Choose a shiny red lipstick that has blue, not orange undertones.
Use a lip brush to apply color evenly. Applying this color lipstick can look dated if it appears too thick on the lips.

The Secret to Hiding Dark Circles

It seems that a model never gets enough sleep, between early calls and very late nights. It's a problem that calls for this 5 step solution.

1. Add a small amount of yellow eye shadow to concealer or foundation.
2. Use a brush or your ring finger and apply this mixture over moisturizer.
3. Start beneath the inner corner of your eye and spread above outer corner. Don't forget to include the area under the lower lashes.
4. Set with pressed powder.
5. Apply foundation and complete makeup

Model Spoon Trick

Carefully hold a clean spoon against the upper eyelid with the hollow side turned in, and the bottom edge lined up with the base of your lashes. Apply mascara using short quick strokes. This trick will prevent mascara from clumping because the extra product will end up on the spoon.

Insider Concealer Trick

Prepare the area with a drop of moisturizer mixed with a drop or two of eye redness reliever. Next take a small brush and dip into concealer. Gently brush over blemish or other imperfection.

Insider Tip

Models get their eye shadow to stay on through several shows by applying foundation to their lids, then powder, and then mixing cream and powder shadow together before application.

Model Hair

Models change their hair almost as often as they change outfits. Almost all models color their hair to enhance their complexions and add volume.

Models have learned to rely on hair stylists. Their stylists change so often that it's a certainty that their looks change often and remain fresh.

Models Feed Their Hair

Models not only deep condition their hair weekly, they rely on vitamins that directly nourish the hair.

Cod liver oil

B complex

Biotin

Runway Hair

This is an easy technique used to create an "at the beach" funky look.

Use any clear carbonated soda (like Sprite).

Pour about a cup into a spray bottle.

Spritz on the end of curly or wavy hair and scrunch the ends while blow drying.

Bring hair back to life by rolling it in the opposite direction of the style.

Hair Prevention

Stylists keep models' hair from denting by slipping a tissue under hair clips when applying makeup.

Keep a comb between your flat iron and scalp to prevent burning.

To keep your hair style fresh, wrap a towel around your head before heading to the shower. Put your shower cap over the towel. This prevents any humidity from getting into your hair.

Fat Hair

1. Switch your part to the opposite side and you'll create instant volume.
2. Comb styling gel through slightly damp hair. Twist sections around your finger and hold them in place with clips.
3. Blow dry on a low setting, remove clips, and lift hair at roots with your fingers.
4. Add instant volume to short hair by working mousse through hair, then drying with a diffuser.
5. Make long hair look thicker by bending over at the waist and brushing forward. This injects air into the roots and makes them stand up. Use hair spray at the root for even more lift.

Model Eating

Aspiring models are taught healthy ways of staying as thin as necessary to stay in the industry. Trust me, model eating is not just diet soda and bubble gum. No they don't always listen, and try to short cut their way to the perfect body. I've seen it all, both from the vantage point of a model and their trainer. The models who stay in their careers the longest are the ones who know that what they put into their bodies will eventually show up on the outside.

Salsa

A model's favorite snack at every photo shoot is without a doubt salsa. Salsa is a snack that is low in calories (a mere 10 calories for two heaping tablespoons), and is full of antioxidants. Models prefer the extra hot stuff since it makes them drink lots of water, a must for keeping their bodies detoxified and their skin glowing.

Tea

Models drink tea for beauty and health! Green and black tea contains fluoride and polyphenols to prevent plaque from adhering to the tooth's surface. Green tea helps to speed up the metabolism and prevent wrinkles.
Models rely on dandelion tea as a diuretic, found in whole foods stores.

Model Body Tricks

Model Stance

Keep weight on one leg, and bring your other leg forward so one foot is crossed in front of the other, then bend your knee slightly to create a slim line.

Longer Legs

Use a flat brush or your finger to trace highlighter or shimmer in a vertical line over shins. Apply a small dab on the tops of knees and on the bones of the ankles and blend. The shimmer creates a line that visually lengthens legs and is often used on the catwalk.

Insider Tip

Sleep in cotton leggings after applying a thick layer of moisturizing lotion. In the morning your legs will be super smooth.

Slimmer Arms

Use a sponge or your finger to "stripe" shimmer down the middle of upper arms. It makes the arm appear longer and slimmer.

Insider Tip

Models use face firming masks to tighten their arms. Apply the mask to the back of the arms and allow to dry.
Remove by rubbing briskly off with a vegetable or loofah brush.

Runway Legs

To legs look instantly tan rub hair serum mixed with bronzing powder evenly all over legs. This highlights the bones and creates definition.
If there's time for self tanner, mix it with a small amount of moisturizer for an even look.

Insider Tip

When models have an assignment and tend to break out, they take one or two antacid tablets before going to bed.
The antacid balances the acid in the skin and helps to prevent a breakout.

Disguise a Nose Bump

Some models have slight bumps that can easily be disguised. After applying foundation, dip a brush into a slightly darker concealer than your skin tone. Run the concealer down the bridge of the nose. On the side of each nostril draw a light line with a light bronzer.

Model Body Tools

Face Training

Models use surgical tape (available at drugstores) to smooth skin while sleeping and preventing furrows. We make expressions during sleep that are uncontrollable and can cause permanent wrinkling. Tape an "X" between your eyebrows just above your nose to duplicate this trick.

Gaffers or Duct Tape

Anything that needs tacking down on a photo shoot, this will do the job. Some models have even been known to tape their tummies down with it.

Toupee Tape

Use it to keep a plunging neckline from becoming front page news. It keeps bra straps from becoming unsightly and generally keeping anything lightweight adhered to your body. I like it because it's meant to stick to skin, not a pipe.

Double Stick Carpet Tape

It is used for lots of clothing calamities, like drooping buttons, hem holding, appliqué sticking, and handbag embellishment. It is also useful for holding belt ends in place.

Clear Eyelash Adhesive

You can do everything from holding a flimsy strap close to the skin to keeping jewelry from dangling around.

Golf Grip Tape

Also called "butt glue" because it keeps swimsuits from riding up, it also helps to secure a strapless top, and keep ankle wrap sandals from moving around.

Take a Model Photo

The first trick that a model learns is how to take a great picture. They can be beautiful in person but if they can't get it across in a photo then there is no career. You can use these same tips to look fabulous in every photo you take. As you may have found out, the worst pictures seem to last the longest.

Makeup

Don't use moisturizer under your foundation. It can look "greasy" in a photo.
Use extra powder, but make sure it's matte not translucent for best results.
If flash photography is used, go heavier than usual with your makeup.
Avoid frosts or odd colors.

Colors

Black is not always the best color because it can bring out under eye circles and shadows.
White washes your complexion out. Choose vibrant primary colors, and avoid faded pastels.
Avoid patterns which grab too much attention away from the face.

Turn Your Head Slightly

By turning your head slightly to the side you make your face appear slimmer.
When you do so, be sure to look slightly up. It will create a better angle and flatter your profile.

Lift your Elbows

Take your elbows away from your body. Having them hang by your sides makes your arms look like they're part of your body and subsequently adds weight.

Lean and Step

Place one foot in front of the other and lean back from the camera. This lengthens the body and creates a leaner look.

Models Rely on the Tongue Trick

To avoid a double chin in your next picture, press your tongue to the roof of your mouth when you pose. By doing this you will not be able to drop your chin

Model Trick for a Natural Look

Often we need to show a model in a "natural" look.   Yet the conundrum is that we need to use some makeup on even the freshest of faces. Otherwise the features will appear bland and non descript. To infuse natural color into the lips, pout at the mirror. Pull the lower lip down. Then choose a color that most matches the lightest shade of the of middle of your bottom lip.

Replicate that color to accentuate both cheeks and eyes.

Model Regimes
Learn from the Industry's Best!

Veronica Webb
This model and journalist runs once a day and rollerblades twice a week.

Stella Tenant
This nineties super model keeps her complexion radiant by washing only with a half teaspoon glycerin (available at drugstores) and rose water.

Elle Macpherson
Known as the "body", Elle drinks a gallon of water every day. She also eats only twice a day. It's a choice between lunch or dinner, depending on her schedule or mood.

Karen Mulder
This Victoria Secret alumnus takes a daily dose of supplements that include goldenseal root and magnesium.

Alek Wek
The most exotic model to hit the runways since Iman, her skin is darkly pigmented and ashy. Her trick is to rub baby oil all over her legs and arms to give it remarkable glisten , shadowing, and shine.

Gisele Bundchen
The reigning model for several years now, it's impossible to believe that she has any flaws. Gisele applies dark concealer to the tip of her nose to make it appear shorter.

Naomi Campbell
With one of the longest modeling careers in the business, Naomi always brushes her lips each time she brushes her teeth. It keeps the lip area smooth and slightly plumped.

Molly Sims
The model turned actress keeps her weight stable at the age of 34 by snacking on raw almonds during the day.

Tricks of the Trade

Make Your Shoes Slip Proof

To avoid slipping in new shoes do what the models do before walking the runway.
Apply medical tape on the soles.   Medical tape has a rough texture and is easily removable.

Fake Flawless Skin

A small amount of glycerin over the skin is a fabulous foundation primer.
It creates an invisible layer that holds foundation in place while smoothing skin texture.

Chapter 5
Insider Hair

What's the Secret?

Great hair starts with a fabulous cut. Without a great cut, there's nothing you can do with your hair or anything else that will make you feel that your looks are together. Overgrown hair feels heavy and out of balance. Your hair won't do what it's supposed to, it falls back when it should swing to the side. You can't blow dry, gel, or spray your hair into shape.

A good cut can make your face appear slimmer, your flaws less noticeable, and your hair more shiny. Your stylist should address your hair from every angle, work with your head shape, and planes of your face.

If your stylist doesn't spend at least an hour on you then you need to keep searching.

Salon Tips

To get your money's worth and the best possible result, be proactive when you're at the Salon.

1. Don't cross your legs.
2. Sit up straight.
3. Advise your stylist about what chemicals and other treatments you've used on your hair in the past so that she can assess what chemicals she can use without jeopardizing your hair condition.

How to Care for Your Hair

No Plastic Bristles!

Every stylist I have worked with agrees on this☐The proper bristles make the difference in not only how your style comes out, but the condition your hair keeps. Purchase a boar bristle in a round or flat brush to use on dry hair. If you want a separate brush to work with damp hair, then a soft rubber toothed widely spaced brush is best. Using a brush with boar bristles also reduces frizz.

Always Brush Before Shampooing

It's important to give your hair a gentle brushing before shampooing. It breaks up residue and dandruff flakes as well as distributes oils to aid your shampoo & conditioning routine.

Shampoo Your Way to Great Hair

The first step to perfect shampooing is to pour the shampoo into the palms of your hands, not straight from the bottle. Apply the shampoo into the strands of the hair and not directly to the scalp. Shampoo will weigh down the roots, so use lather only on the scalp itself.

Insiders Tip

Take the time to stimulate the scalp and encourage hair growth by massaging your scalp for a few minutes when you shampoo.

Blow Drying

1. After washing and conditioning, blot out excess moisture by gently patting your hair with an absorbent towel.
2. Divide hair into four parts and clip.
3. Start drying at the back of the head, pulling two inch sections out, holding it with a big round brush.
4. Aim the dryer down over the top of the hair to avoid frizz.
5. After hair has dried, apply serum or hair spray.

Note If you wear bangs, always blow dry them first.

Insiders Tip

Dry hair faster by using a metal core brush when blow drying. The metal will retain heat for a faster finish.

Insider Coloring

Wet the ends of your hair with warm water before you color. The ends of your hair are more porous so this is the way to prevent uneven coloring. Wet hair won't absorb hair color as dry hair will.

Don't color freshly washed hair. Your hair's natural oils will help your color to adhere better. Let your hair rest for at least a day or two before coloring. Make sure you don't have any product in your hair which could result in uneven coloring.

Tip: Use a deep conditioning treatment a few days before coloring. The strands will be less porous and will absorb dye better.

If you are buying kits and your hair is very thick or longer than shoulder length you need to purchase two kits.

Tip: Rub a cotton ball soaked in Sea Breeze along the hair line or anywhere else color needs to be removed.

Preserve Your Color

To prevent your hair from discoloring, rinse your hair with warm water before swimming. Hair that is wet won't be able to absorb chlorinated water.

Moisturize your hair if you're going to be out in the sun and can't wear a hat.

Pat your colored hair, don't rub it when you towel dry. Vigorous towel drying damages your hair's delicate cuticle, making it look dull and prone to breaking.

Treat your colored hair with a deep conditioner at least once a week since colored hair tends to be dry.

Getting Back to Your Natural Color

There's more to getting back to the color you were born with than just letting it grow out. You may not remember what your natural color is anymore. The best way to match back to nature is to pull your hair back to expose the roots. Choose coloring that is close to that color. If you can wait and switch gradually by having your stylist blend in low lights then this may be the best way to go. It will probably take only three appointments.

Product Build up Remover

Combine a bottle of water, 2 tablespoons of lemon juice, and ½ cup of Epsom Salt.
Let solution set overnight. Apply to dry hair and let set for 10 minutes and shampoo out.

Shine Enhancer

Chamomile tea gives shine to the hair and takes away brassiness.
Brew 2 teabags in a cup of boiling water. Allow to cool and use as a final rinse.

Treat Extremely Damaged Hair

When hair is severely damaged, it is necessary to use a treatment before shampooing. A hot oil treatment will be most successful. Use extra virgin olive oil warmed in the microwave.

Fight Dandruff

Insiders use tea tree oil to get rid of dandruff. It's a natural and inexpensive solution that not only cures dandruff but alleviates an itchy scalp. You can purchase tea tree oil at most drugstores and health food stores. Apply a few drops to the scalp before shampooing. Massage it in for a few minutes and then shampoo and condition.

Fight Hair Static

Use Static Guard on your hair when you absolutely do not want frizzies.
A very small amount is advised, so the best way to apply it is to spray a small amount in the palm of your hand, rub palms together, and then pat lightly over the hair shaft.
Stiff bristles can make hair more static. Soften bristles (especially round brush bristles) with heat from your blow dryer first.

Shine On!

If you color your hair you can maintain the shine of the processed color by using color-protective products. Loss of shine can also be caused by product build up. Too much heat caused by over styling (flat ironing, blow drying at high heat, etc.) can also cause hair to become dull.

1. Don't over process your hair. Color only when absolutely necessary.
2. Use low heat when styling your hair.
3. Read the ingredient label and try to avoid products that contain alcohol.
4. Spritz your hair with a protective product before blow drying.
5. Use a hot oil treatment at least once a week to add healthy shine.

Healthy Hair

Hair is over 90 per cent protein, and when that protein is broken down by the elements, it leads to damage. Coconut oil is the insiders remedy. It was found in a recent issue of the Journal of Cosmetic Science to be far superior to mineral and sunflower oil. They cannot penetrate the hair shaft and bond like coconut oil.

Don't bother paying a lot for products containing coconut oil. Get it in its pure form at health food stores or natural supermarkets. Apply it to dry hair and allow to set for at least 30 minutes before shampooing.

Trim Your Own Bangs

It's not necessary to run to the salon each time your bangs need a little trim. Stylists have been trimming model's hair with these steps.

1. Grasp a small section of hair with your fingers. If your bangs are cut styled straight across then keep your fingers horizontal. If they are slanted your fingers should be slanted in the same way.
2. Use small scissors to get optimum control.
3. Don't cut across your forehead. Instead hold the scissors vertically, and cut into the bangs. It creates a softer look.
4. Snip a quarter inch off each section. You can go back and trim more later after you've combed your bangs out.
5. Start at the center of your forehead and trim outward until you reach the middle of your eyebrow. Then repeat with the other side.
6. Be careful not to cut past your eyebrows which could create a hole.

Hair Product Application

Hair Gel
Apply gel to only slightly dampened, not wet hair.

Hair Spray
When using spray leave at least a six inch clearance to prevent matting the hair down and creating a "shell" look.

Mousse
Apply mousse only on the roots. It will weigh the rest of the hair down, especially the ends.

Chapter 6
Beauty on the Run

There's Always Time for Beauty

Even if you have five minutes (or less!) there's no reason to go out the door looking like you just got out of bed. The intent is to make a major impact with a minimal amount of time and effort.

Create a Quick Face

Take three steps and make them one to save precious time.

Choose a cream to powder foundation. It acts as a foundation, concealer, and setting powder in one step.

Use ivory eye shadow to highlight your cheekbones, brow bone, and to highlight the center of your lips.

Mix together blush and bronzer and apply at once.

Insider Tip

The best makeup brushes insure the easiest fastest application. Make sure your set of brushes include a fan brush.

Two Minute Face

If you have just two minutes to make up your face, then choose bronzer.

Apply it to your eyes to define.

Mix it with petroleum jelly to use on lips.

Use it on cheeks, on the sides of the nose, forehead, and chin.

One Minute Face

Swipe concealer on any trouble spots and blend.

Pencil the outer corners of the eye.

Spread sheer lip gloss which doesn't require precise application.

In a rush, don't bother with a full eye makeup application; line only the outer corners of your eye with a cream eye liner.

Quick Firming

Use the white of an egg to firm up sagging areas of the face temporarily.

Dip your fingers into an unbeaten egg white and gently pat on skin. Don't move a muscle until the egg white dries. If a white coating appears after drying, you've applied too much. Wet your index finger and gently lift off excess.

Hair in a Hurry

Save time by using shampoo that contains conditioner in one application.

If you have literally seconds, then blow dry only your bangs and pull the rest back.

Use hair accessories when you don't have time to tend to your hair at all.

A ponytail is a girl's best friend for beauty on the run.

Hair gel is a lightening quick way to look put together. Just rub a little in the palms of your hands and slick it all back. You're good to go with shining style.

Insider Tip

For quick flowing locks, twist damp hair into evenly divided ringlets, then spritz with hair spray. Finish dressing, making up, etc., and then untwist hair and finger comb out.

Speedy Shine

Use a shine enhancer to coat the cuticle of the hair. The result is that it will immediately reflect light on the hair shaft, creating a glossy sheen.

No Work Nails

Clear or light colored polish is the quickest way to do your nails and keep them looking finished with little effort.

If there's absolutely no time for a manicure, apply a coat of ridge filler. It has a milky texture and creamy color that mimics a pale colored polish and dries very quickly.

Smooth ragged cuticles with oil.

Exercise on the Run

Even when you're on the road you can still work out.

Face Firming

While you're driving, or in the privacy of your office, try to reach your nose with your tongue. You most likely won't be able to do this (unless you're Gene Simmons of KISS), but the effort will firm up your jaw line and diminish jowling. It also helps to minimize a double chin. While you're reaching, hold to the count of ten. Repeat 10 to 15 times a day.

Better Posture

Here's another exercise that works well in the car. Adjust your shoulder blades so that they are touching the back of your seat. Hold to the count of ten. Do this at least ten times a day.

Calf Strengthening

We all know that wearing heels work your calves throughout the day, but here's a good way to do an effective calf workout while standing in line. Simply raise your legs until you're almost on your tip toes. Hold to the count of 15. Lower and repeat 5 more times. That line suddenly won't seem so very long.

A Better Butt

Here's a quick and convenient way to work on everyone's favorite problem area. When you have a spare moment, whether you're standing in line or stuck in traffic, contract your buttocks and hold tight for 15 seconds. Not only will you firm your butt but this move also helps to relieve stress.

The Car Dance

You can work your abs on the road in a move I call the Car Dance. Concentrate on your rib cage and try to duplicate the moves of an exotic dancer.

Fast Beauty Tricks

Instant Face Lift

Gather a large amount of hair into a pony tail at the crown. Adhere with a hair accessory or elastic band. Tease the pony tailed area for fullness, lightly smoothing with a brush. When you lift your hair this way, you are pulling your face up too.

Quick Cheekbones

Apply bronzer underneath the cheekbone and along the jaw line.
Use a smaller contour brush rather than a fluffy blush brush.
Be careful to blend out lines.
Finish with a light pink blush on the apples of the cheeks.

Fuller Lips

Just switch from a matte to a shimmery gloss.
Swipe it over your regular lipstick.
If you use a light gloss, you can extend it slightly beyond the lip line and don't need to be exact.

Big Eyes

Dab a small amount of beige eye shadow on the center of your eyelids.
Blend slightly with the warmth of your pinky finger.

Long Lasting Lips

Use dry blush to seal lips.
Apply a small dot with your finger and smudge over moisturized lips.
Start in the center and work to the edges.

Cover Blemishes

A creamy nude pencil will quickly cover flaws and dark areas.
An alternative is to apply translucent powder by pressing down on the blemish.

Fast & Flawless Skin

If you didn't have time for a facial, and your skin is looking pallid or parched rely on the insider's favorite, witch hazel.

Apply it to clean, dry skin with a cotton ball. Witch hazel immediately shrinks pores and temporarily tightens skin.

Follow up with foundation and makeup.

Substitute bronzer for face powder to further hide imperfections.

Fast Fashion

How can you look fashionable with the least amount of care in your clothing? It's possible with the new fabrics that are now available.

1. Choose acrylic over wool and cashmere. Acrylic fabrics have come a long way in the past few years. They are now softer and often referred to as "faux cashmere". It looks just like the real thing without the cost or care. Acrylic is highly resilient, and can be machine washed and comes out of the dryer ready to wear. It rarely needs ironing.

2. Polyester is no longer the cheap stuff from the disco era. It mimics silk and no one has to be the wiser. The thinner fabrics look the best.

Chapter 7
Insider Dieting

Meet the Super Foods

There are beauty boosters courtesy of nature that are a "must" in the world of insiders who respect the correlation and response of food to their looks. These foods are the consummate "eating for beauty".

Broccoli

At only 25 calories a serving, you get a tremendous amount of wrinkle fighting antioxidants and cancer fighters.

Turkey Breast

This lean protein helps your body turn fat into muscle. More muscle tissue helps to keep your metabolism fired up.

Beans

The University of Kentucky researchers found that subjects who ate a daily serving of cooked beans every day lost more than two pounds in three weeks without any dieting. Beans contain more than seven grams of fiber per serving.

Shrimp

At just 84 calories and one fat gram per serving, shrimp is a super lean protein that not only builds muscle but stops hunger. Protein like shrimp takes longer to digest than carbohydrates, keeping you full for a longer period. Instead of cocktail sauce, choose salsa.

Cucumbers

Because of their high water content, cucumbers act as a diuretic in the body, flushing out retained water.
Their high fiber content helps to curb hunger and transport fat and calories out of the body.

Egg Whites

Very lean proteins like egg whites are rich in L-Carnitine which unlocks fat stored in the body's cells and helps it to be burned for energy.

Grapefruit

One of the most popular foods of insiders, studies have shown that citrus fruits like grapefruit have a lipotropic effect on the body, prompting the body to burn more fat.

Popcorn

Three cups of air popped popcorn is filled with satisfying fiber and low in calories. The carbs are immediately turned into energy, and it's the number one snack of insider beauties like Madonna.

Whole Grain Bread

Every slice of whole grain bread contains 85 micrograms of chromium which suppresses sweet cravings and allows the body to shed stored fat.

Cook Like an Insider

Roast your vegetables to bring out their natural sweetness. Peel and cut them into two inch pieces and roast them at 375 degrees. Be sure to coat the bottom of the pan so they won't stick. Keep them in the frig and microwave them briefly when you get an urge for something sweet.

Use herbs and spices to give foods a flavor boost. Naomi Campbell, Gisele, and other well known insider beauties carry their own spices while on the road.
1. Toast spices to further intensify their flavors
2. Add spices to cooking liquids

Forget high fat salad dressings, do what insiders do, and use flavored vinegars on fish, grains, salads, and vegetables. From zero to five calories a serving, vinegar is a maximum flavor boost with no guilt.

Sugar & Wrinkles

If consumed in excess researchers state that sugar can accelerate skin wrinkling.
Excess sugar molecules attach themselves to collagen fibers causing them to lose strength and flexibility. The result is that skin becomes not only less elastic, but more vulnerable to sun damage, sagging, and wrinkling.

Note□Excess sugar is defined as over ten teaspoons a day.

Beware of Too Much Salt

Although everyone needs salt, it can cause problems with your diet. Watch how much you get in your diet. Even diet soda has sodium so read your labels. Fast food is another culprit.

Don't Be Afraid of Coffee

A little coffee is a good thing! You see the insiders photographed with their faithful java in their hands daily. Don't chock it up to another bad habit. There's value in that cup.

Coffee Fights Cavities

The ingredient that gives coffee its aroma and taste has both antibacterial and anti adhesive properties. What does this mean? Cavities can't stick! This comes from an extensive Italian study where those smiles shine bright from behind those beautiful bronze faces.

Coffee Is a Workout Enhancer

If you drink coffee before exercising you'll find yourself working out both longer and harder. Researchers at the Nutrition and Food Science Division of Drexel University of Philadelphia have discovered that caffeine stimulates the release of endorphins, hormones that lower the sensation of pain or discomfort, which in turn lessens fatigue.

Coffee Makes You Feel Good

John Hopkins School of Medicine reports that drinking a cup of coffee increases your sense of well being, boosts energy, makes you more alert, and engenders self confidence.

Too Much Coffee
(That means more than 3 cups a day)
1. Can reduce fertility (cause sluggish sperm)
2. Can be bad for bones (being a diuretic, it can push vitamins out of your body)

Make It Taste Better
We have found that making foods that are low in calories to taste better helps insiders reach and attain their goals.

Add a little cinnamon to cereal, coffee, yogurt and even toast for a no calorie treat and a metabolism booster.

Keep cucumber slices on the kitchen counter. Dip them in mustard or wasabi sauce to quickly satisfy your need to munch. Plan to eat a whole cucumber each day, and be sure to include the peel for an extra fiber boost.

Slim with Scents
There are scents that have the ability to stop hunger dead in its tracks. At the top of the list is the prickly pear. Studies at the Smell & Taste Treatment and Research Foundation in Chicago have found that inhaling this scent activates the brain's satiety center, greatly reducing calorie intake.

If you have difficulty find prickly pear, don't worry. Other effective scents include lemon and orris root available at grocery stores.

Lose Weight with Tea
Hawthorn berry tea (available at health food stores and natural supermarkets) is a natural diuretic that curbs the appetite while flushing out fat cells. Drink two cups a day for best results.

Insiders Eat Well

They only allow high quality foods to pass their lips. Highly processed products don't merit their list, and their idea of junk food is a cupboard full of the highest quality snacks.

You will find a higher degree of satisfaction if you purchase the best products you can afford. If you can't afford Dom Perignon, stock up your liquor cabinet with demi bottles of champagne. There will be little waste and will give you a feeling of luxury with limited calories (75 calories for a glass of champagne) and well within your budget.

Consider placing a standing order with your favorite grocer. This usually doesn't cost anything extra, and you'll be assured of always having the freshest cuts. If you are a regular customer you may even be able to get free delivery. It's a feeling of decadence that will not leave you feeling deprived. Doing this will insure that you continually have the right foods ready at all times.

Insiders Eat by Intuition

They listen to their bodies to tell them what and when to eat.

Turn your dinner meal into your breakfast. Not everyone likes breakfast food and consequently will skip this important meal.

Cameron Diaz is a perfect example of this and it has served her body well. She eats chicken with salsa as her breakfast meal each morning. The benefit of doing this is a big dose of protein in the morning gets the metabolism fired up to burn more calories throughout the day.

Insiders Stop Eating After the "Sigh"

When you feel the urge to take a deep breath or to let out a sigh, it's a signal to stop eating. Your body is telling you that you are full.

It also works if you deliberately stop to take a deep breath after every few bites. This slows down your eating and makes you more relaxed during your meal.

Insider's Favorite Diets

Raw Food Diet
This diet is favored by celebrities like Alicia Silverstone and Demi Moore.
90 per cent of your diet must be uncooked. Everything you eat must be raw until dinner.
On this diet you can only eat fruit on an empty stomach and must eat every three hours.
There's no calorie counting.

The Zone
Stars like Jennifer Aniston keep trim on this diet where you eat three pre-packaged meals and
two snacks a day. It's expensive if you get the meals delivered, but incredibly easy if you are
uncomfortable keeping food in your home. Drinking at least eight glasses of water is important
on the Zone as well as eating every five hours.

The Hamptons Diet
Renee Zellweger, Kate Hudson, and Sarah Jessica Parker reportedly are all followers of this
diet which is based on the Mediterranean Diet. It includes lots of vegetables and low fat fruits
like blueberries. Fatty fish like salmon and haddock are included for the beneficial omega-3
fatty acids. Also recommended is the use of macadamia oil as the main cooking oil because it
has up to 30 percent more monounsaturated fat than olive oil. Plus it does not oxidize as
quickly and lose nutrients.

Insider Tip
A cough drop containing menthol or eucalyptus stimulates your taste buds and sends a
satisfaction signal to your brain, quickly ending your cravings.

Don't Be Afraid of Bread
The very thought of bread has for too long filled dieters with dread.
Now that the hype on Protein diets has died down, it's time to reveal the virtues of bread.

It Feeds Your Brain

The starch in bread is the brain's source of fuel. Eating whole grain bread will greatly slow down your cravings for cookies and pasta.

Stops Hunger Pains

The whole grains in high quality breads will slowly digest in your body and keep blood sugar levels steady. At only 40 to 45 calories per slice, light breads are a wonderful low calorie snack.

Bread Keeps You Happy

If you're satisfied, and your serotonin levels remain high, then dieting becomes just so much easier.

Bread is Actually a Health Food

Eating the right kind of bread controls blood sugar and even lowers cholesterol levels.

Bread is a Tranquilizer

Too much protein can cause jitters. Eating a slice of bread can calm your nerves. Anxiety eating can be quelled by a slice of whole grain bread.

A little bread keeps your serotonin levels high, which keep cravings for a quick sweet fix at bay. A slice of high protein bread when cravings are calling can help suppress them.

Insider Eating Out Tricks

When you reach a point where you're feeling satisfied, and slowing down, take your napkin and place it over your plate. It would be just too embarrassing to remove the napkin and start eating again.

Drink a glass or two of water before your meal comes.

Sip coffee or tea with your meal to slow your eating down.

Give some food away before you begin your meal.

Choosing red wine is a calorie friendly choice at just 75 calories a glass.

Curb Your Cravings.

Sniff Away Your Cravings

Researchers have found that sniffing peppermint or green apple can suppress hunger. It's not necessary to carry a peppermint candy or a big apple in your purse.
You can find small vials of these scents at most health food stores.

Combine Hot and Cold

One of the favorite ways insider curb cravings is to combine a hot drink like coffee or tea with a cold fruit. Ideal for filling you up is to have a cup of green tea with a cold crisp apple.

Write Everything Down

Keep a journal of each bite you put in your mouth. You don't have to count calories, but at the end of the day when you look at that list you'll be able to see where you've been virtuous as well as all your mistakes.

Use the Internet for Support

There are groups all over the internet and can work whenever you feel that your willpower is starting to dip. You'll find inspiration, dieting buddies, and exchange recipes.

Add Vinegar

Insiders have long used vinegar as a dieting tool. Not only does it add flavor, but vinegar increases feelings of fullness. Studies have also been done to indicate that it reduces fat storage and lowers disease risk. According to research from the European Journal of Clinical Nutrition, vinegar is an effective way to accelerate weight loss.

Snack on Protein

A great way to take the edge off between meals is with a protein snack. Keep cheese and hard boiled eggs in the frig so that it's readily at hand.

Salt Creates False Weight

Cutting down on salt can create a five pound weight loss. Salt retains excess fluid.

Drink like the French

Red wine is the drink of choice by elegant thin French women. An antioxidant found in red wine only has been found by researchers to boost the body's ability to break down fats.

Bloat Deflators

1. Water
2. Exercise
3. Eating fresh and not from a package or can
4. Foods without a lot of preservatives

Cut Fat Cells with Kidney Beans

University of Scranton research has shown that taking an extract made from white kidney beans before eating starchy foods, such as potatoes and pastas will stop an enzyme in your body from converting those starches into sugar. The results are that fewer sugar calories will be stored as fat cells.

Recommended dosage: 1,200 mg

Shirataki Noodles

An insider diet secret that has long been used in Japan, shirataki noodles contain a mere 40 calories a serving and absolutely zero fat. These noodles are also rich in Glucomannan, allowing them to literally expand in the stomach. The result is that you will feel full and satisfied on fewer calories.

Find them in your local supermarket (usually in the international aisle) or find an Asian supermarket.

Chapter 8
Maintain & Organize

Protect Your Important Investments

You can't truly be in control of your looks unless you're in control of your stuff. That includes your makeup, your wardrobe, and even your purse. You've paid good money for your things, and it makes sense to keep them in good repair. It doesn't take long, and helps to keep everything around you organized. It will make life easier for you in the long run. Once you know how to care for your things, you'll save money by extending the life of everything you own.

Clean Out the Clutter

Organize

Keep only your most flattering pieces in your closet. The old adage of throwing out what you haven't worn in a year is a good one, but not across the board. I prefer that you conduct an inventory at the end of every season. Ask yourself, "Did I wear it this season?" "Did it go with more than one item?" "Did I receive any compliments?" These questions are a good barometer as to the value of the piece. If you can't answer yes to at least two of these questions, ditch it.

So What Are You Going to Do with Your Cast Offs?

1. Find a resale store and put it on consignment and make some money.
2. Sell it on EBay if it's in excellent condition.
3. Donate it charity. Don't forget to get a receipt for a tax deduction.
4. Toss it or use it as a rag if it's not in such good shape that you would give to a friend.

Keep Clothes Like New

1. Close the closet door. Some fabrics fade or streak when exposed to light.
2. Don't wash or dry clean unless necessary. Each time you do, you lessen the life of the fabric.
3. Never store clothing in plastic. Fabrics need to "breathe".

Hang Ups

Create More Room

A crowded closet is a guaranteed wrinkle creator. Button up jackets and blouses. Zip up zippers, and hang pants down from the waist or cuffs.

Hang clothes by category, outfit, or possibilities.

No More Wire Hangers

Make your own padded hangers with old shoulder pads. Just pin them to wire hangers. This will eliminate unsightly ridges appearing.

Keep clothing from slipping off by wrapping a rubber band around each end of the hanger. The rubber band will "grab" the material to keep the garment secure.

Make your own skirt hanger by adding clothespins to any hanger.

Insider Tip

Coat wooden hangers with a few coats of clear nail polish to prevent clothing from getting snagged on rough edges.

Jackets

Hang all jackets and coats on heavy wooden hangers that can support their weight. Otherwise your garments will sag and lose their shape. Keep all items buttoned or zipped.

Shoulder Surgery

To quickly remove "shoulder bumps" from a blouse or sweater, sprinkle water on the bumps. Then, with the setting on high, use a hair dryer and direct air flow on the bumpy spots. The heat will loosen the warped fibers so that the fabric settles back into its original shape.

Swim Suit Care & Cleaning

Right after swimming, rinse suit out in cool water. If you have any creams, oils, sunscreen or lotion on your suit, use shampoo to sponge it off.

Wash suit in a gentle detergent or baby shampoo. Regular detergents can harm swimsuit fabrics.

Block dry your suit. Do not put it in the dryer.

Always hand wash your suits, because a washing machine will cause a suit to become misshapen.

Cleaning

Save on Dry cleaning

Toss your dry cleanables in the dryer with a towel dipped in a third of a cup of fabric softener and three quarters cup water for 10 to 15 minutes under very low heat. The heat will release wrinkling while the fabric softener mixture will freshen the fabric.

Whiten whites by adding ½ cup baking soda to your detergent.

Panty Hose Trick

Place an old pair of panty hose in the dryer with dark items. The hose attracts the lint, leaving everything else lint free!

Try to find clothing that has been treated with Teflon. Don't worry, it won't make the garment shiny or uncomfortable, and it will allow stains to fall right off.

Insider Tip

Throw your woolens in the dryer on a cool setting along with a couple of fabric softener sheets every few days. It will freshen and fluff them up. It will also remove moisture from the fabric, which is a magnet for dust mites. Circulating and heating your garments will dislodge small particles from the wool, leaving them allergen free.

Knit Concerns

Turn knits that pill easily inside out before washing.
Remove pilling with a pumice stone, lint brush, or tape.

Leather Care

Soften Stiff Leather

Some new leathers, especially less expensive brands, need to be softened both to look better and be more comfortable. Rub the garment with olive oil. This is especially important with leather pants which tend to "creak".

Make Suede Last Forever!

1. Remove salt as soon as possible and treat with vinegar.
2. Allow wet suede to dry, and then raise the nap with a closely tufted pet brush.
3. Gently blow dry.

Shoe Care

Get your shoes resoled with a rubber bottom and taps. It is will strengthen impact points.
Have your cobbler apply heel shields. They're under five dollars and will protect your heels from scrapes and marks.
Change the shoes you wear from day to day to give them a chance to bounce back. This also lessens the chance our feet will develop corns and calluses in a particular spot.

Insider Tip

Don't place wet shoes near heat unless you need to shrink them.

Patent Leather

Make your patent leather shiny and new by cleaning it with window cleaner and buff with a soft cloth.

Non-Leather

Clean with any all purpose spray. Be sure the cleaner does not contain bleach.

Boots

Keep leather and suede boots from wrinkling by putting an empty egg carton in each leg.
Stuff crumpled newspapers into boots that need reshaping.
The trick is to crumple the newspaper into very small pieces and using as much as you can
possibly fit into the boot.

Stain Solutions

Chalk Removes Stains

Get rid of stains around the collar with white chalk
Rub briskly over the stained area. Let it set for about ten minutes, then launder as usual. The
chalk absorbs the oil that holds onto the dirt, causing the ring.

Fix Bleach Marks

If you have a bleach spot on a black or dark brown garment, fill it in with a permanent black or
brown marker.

Scorch Marks

If you've accidentally scorched an item while ironing, there is hope. Lay a wet cloth over the
spot and iron over it a few times. The mark will disappear. It may be necessary to peel the
scorch mark off.

White Shirt Stains

Stretch the stained portion over an empty cup. Pour white vinegar through the shirt into the
cup.
Wash as usual.

Blood

Rub in full strength household ammonia. Rinse promptly. Never use on silk or woolens.

Butter

Blot with a non-acetone polish remover. Then rinse quickly with cool water.

Chocolate

Stretch fabric over a bowl and secure with a rubber band. Sprinkle Borax over the stain then pour very hot water over it in a circle. Start at the outer edge and end in the center. Wash as usual.

Coffee Stains

Mix one teaspoon white vinegar with one teaspoon dishwashing detergent. Brush on fabric. Wash with detergent that contains a large amount of bleach.

Crayon/Ink

Place item stain side down and spray with WD-40. Let it set for several minutes, then turn over and use on stained side. Gently work in dishwashing detergent. Machine wash using a detergent with color safe bleach.

Lipstick

Wet a baby wipe with vinegar and dab spot away.

Grass

Sponge with two teaspoons cold water mixed with one teaspoon rubbing alcohol. Rinse and launder.

Gravy

Rinse with equal parts of ammonia and water until the stain disappears.

Gum

Dab with ice to harden the gum, then scrape away as much as possible.
Launder in cold water to remove any remaining residue.

Ink

Saturate the stain with hair spray.   Place a towel under the stain and blot. Launder as usual.
Use a bleach enhanced detergent.

Mildew

To get rid of mildew stains, sponge the stained area with lemon juice. Then place the item in
the sun for at least an hour.

Oil & Grease Stains

Treat a grease stain with talcum powder or cornstarch. Sprinkle it on the stain and allow it to
set for 15 minutes.
Brush off the powder and wash.

Rub in petroleum jelly. Rub off excess. Finish by washing in warm soapy water.

Paint

Apply a small amount of paint thinner. Rinse immediately with cool water and wash as usual.
Use a fragranced dryer sheet to soften any remaining residue.

Perspiration

Add 4 tablespoons salt to one quart of hot water. Sponge area. Wash as usual.

Insider Tip

Apply hair spray, perfume, or deodorant at least five minutes before dressing to allow these
products time to dry.
Chemicals can ruin fabrics.

Jewelry Care

Keep your Gems Sparkling

If it's a precious metal use a jewelry cleaner, if not clean with a soft cloth and a small amount of soap and water.

Boil ½ cup ammonia based cleaner with one cup water. Use this solution to clean gold, silver, and platinum.

Try not to get the setting too wet.

Dissolve two denture cleanser tablets in one cup very hot water. Soak all your jewelry safely. Rinse and brush clean with a tooth brush, and wipe with a soft cloth.

In a pinch you can revitalize your gold pieces with a pencil eraser. The rubber particles in an eraser will absorb smudges. Gently rub over the piece a few times until clean.

Brush your jewelry with baking soda or toothpaste.

Insider Tips

Place a piece of white chalk in your jewelry box. It will help keep costume jewelry from tarnishing by absorbing moisture.

Prevent skin discoloration by applying a thin coat of clear nail polish on the metal links and clasps of your jewelry.

Shoe Care

Erase Shoe Scratches

Apply white vinegar to a soft cloth and dab on shoe scuffs and scratches.
Be sure to wipe again and buff with a clean dry cloth.

Keeping Leathers Shining and Soft

Extra Virgin Olive Oil is a natural leather shiner and softener favored by wardrobe stylists.
Use it on leather belts, shoes, boots, and handbags. Stylists prefer olive oil over colored polish since too much polish can build up and dull fine leather.
Wet a soft absorbent cloth and rub briskly into the leather.

Shoe Solutions

Use an eyeliner pencil to fix shoe scuffs.
Rub a cotton ball doused with nail polish remover over black marks.
An old fashion rubber eraser removes grime from sued and fabric shoes.
Dampen a sponge in white vinegar and gently blot away salt stains.
Erase dark marks from pale leather by dabbing with nail polish remover.

Insider Tip

Blot grease stains with a paper towel, and then massage in talcum powder. Brush off with a soft brush.

Prevent Patent Leathers from Cracking

Protect patent leather from weather elements and keep it shining by apply a dab of petroleum jelly with a soft cloth.

Chapter 9
Personal Beauty

Beauty Starts At Home

Unless you're feeling fabulous from head to toe, inside and out, your beauty regime is not complete. The most important beauty routines begin before any clothing or cosmetics are adorned. Every insider beauty I know considers their private beauty routines their own personal spa time. It's an important step in feeling beautiful inside so that it can be reflected on the outside. Think of it as a respite from the world to allow you the confidence to face anything and everything!

Consider personal and intimate beauty care as a respite from the world. It will allow you the inner confidence to face anything and everything that comes your way.

Benefits of Bathing

Many insiders prefer relaxing in a tub. Bathing has the ability to relieve menstrual cramps, aid sleep, and even lift depression. These benefits can be achieved in as little as ten minutes. If you have time, light some candles, put on your favorite music, and let the beauty enhancements begin. The payback will be evident inside and out!

Watch the Temperature

The water in your tub should be warm and comfortable, but not too hot. Water that is too hot drains energy, rather than restore it, and can dry skin out.

A temperature of no more than 110 degrees is most desirable for comfortable bathing.

Before You Step In

Combine two teaspoons of sea salt with one teaspoon vinegar. Massage on dry legs, arms, and buttocks before showering or bathing. Doing this is an effective and simple detox treatment and an effective way of stimulating the lymphatic system. It gives the skin a healthy glow and breaks down cellulite.

Bonus Bathing

Make that soak in the tub even more beneficial by adding elements to fit your specific needs.

Relieve Stress

Brew three cups of very strong chamomile tea and add it to your bath water. Chamomile contains soothing and healing properties that ease away tension.

Energize

Add three or four drops of peppermint to your bath. You can find it in extract or oil form in most supermarkets or health stores.

Insider Tip

Toss a tablet of Alka Seltzer into your tub and your bath will fill up with tiny bubbles to invigorate and soften your skin.

Boost Circulation

Add a cup of cranberry juice under running water and soak for at least twenty minutes.

Relax Your Muscles

Apply a thin film of bath oil over your shoulders and neck, and drop a towel over your shoulders. Let the towel's heat allow the oil to penetrate and relax your muscles.

Insider Tip

Keep two soaps in your bath. You need a deodorant sop for your feet, underarms, genitals, and where you perspire.
Use only mild facial soap for arms, face, and legs. Never use strong soap on those areas.

Revive Dull Skin

Rejuvenate tired skin with an orange juice bath. Simply squeeze the juice of three oranges and pour into very warm water. Soak for 15 to 20 minutes.

Whiter Teeth

You wouldn't believe the lengths that have been reached to get teeth their whitest. In the modeling industry I've seen models use bathroom bleaching cleansers (so dangerous!) to trying to trick the booking agent by applying "White Out" to cover their less than white teeth. Here are some inexpensive, easy, and most of all safe ways to clean and whiten your teeth.

Hydrogen Peroxide

Mix 1/2 teaspoon of hydrogen peroxide with one teaspoon baking soda. It should form a soft paste. Keep adding more baking soda until it does. Use this solution once a week, being careful to avoid your gums. This formula will reduce tarter and remove coffee and wine stains.

Insider Tip

Dip unwaxed dental floss in hydrogen peroxide to bright spaces between teeth where discoloration often starts.

Salt

Mix 3 tablespoons of baking soda with 2 teaspoons salt for a safe and natural cleanser for teeth.

Breath Alert

To keep your breath its freshest be sure to brush your tongue every time you brush your teeth. Your tongue contains lots of bacteria that can contribute to bad breath.

Cozy Up with Tea

The natural chemicals in black and green tea get rid of the bacteria that contribute to bad breath. Boil a strong cup of mint (peppermint, spearmint, etc.) tea. Cool and use as a rinse.

Chew Parsley

It contains tons of chlorophyll, which is the active ingredient in breath mints.

Check Mouthwash Labels
Make sure the ingredients contain antibacterial properties to kill bacteria.

Honey Clove Rinse
Mix ¼ cup honey with one teaspoon of ground gloves. This mouthwash is also good as a sore throat gargle, and can be thinned if desired.

Drink Lots of Water
Make sure you drink plenty of water to wash away bacteria and to encourage saliva production.

Get the Most from Your Perfume
Spray it on the "WARM" parts of your body, the "pulse points. Allow the heat of your body to activate the scent and keep it going for you.

Insider Tip
Never rub perfume on. Allow it soak in.

If you really want your fragrance to last and create the most impact apply fragrance down the chest to the cleavage.

Store your perfume in a cool dark area to help it to retain its potency. Fashionistas I know keep theirs in the frig, the ideal environment to increase longevity. Throw your fragrance out if it begins to smell in any way sour or has the odor of alcohol.

Find Your Scent
1. Hit the perfume counters at midday when your sense of smell is sharpest.
2. Carry coffee beans when you shop for perfume. It "cleanses" the palate for the nose. Some fragrance counters will provide the coffee beans for you. Give the beans a whiff after trying three different scents.
3. Spritz a few choices on paper blotters.

Fragrance Findings

Men estimate women to be 12 pounds thinner when they're wearing a spicy or musky scent. Women appear to be up to six years younger when wearing a vanilla, baby-powder, or grapefruit scent.

Experts Report:

Citrus scents increase alertness by stimulating the irritant nerve in the nose.
Lavender scents calm by boosting alpha wave activity.
Cinnamon and vanilla scents increase arousal.
Honeysuckle scents increase learning speed by boosting brain power.

Getting Rid of Too Much Perfume

If you have gone overboard on your fragrance and there's no time to shower it off, then grab some rubbing alcohol and pour it onto a cotton ball. Gently dab at the areas where you applied your fragrance. This will diffuse the odor and create more mellow tones.

If you want to remove the fragrance, good old soap and water on a small cloth is your answer. If you're out at a party and you feel your scent is too strong, discreetly dip your finger into your cocktail and rub over the scent. The alcohol in your drink will diffuse the strength of your fragrance.

Insider Tip

Keep cosmetic and perfume labels clear by coating them with clear nail polish. The labels can fade over time or smear if they get wet.

Self Tanning

Applying self tanner so that it looks natural takes time and practice. Start by washing skin with a creamy cleanser and shave wherever you are planning to apply tanner.

Exfoliate skin with a soft scrub. Pay attention to rough areas on feet, knees, and elbows. Rinse and dry thoroughly before applying tanner.

Professional Application Techniques

Apply moisturizer to elbows, knees, and feet before applying tanner.

Don't shave legs for several hours before applying sunless tanners.

Rub a thin layer of petroleum jelly around your nails, and between your fingers and toes to protect that area of the skin.

If using a spray hold the nozzle approximately six inches from the skin. Spray from the feet up in small circles.

Don't apply tanner to tops of feet, elbows, or knees.

When using lotion, work a quarter size dollop from feet to neck in horizontal and then vertical strokes.
If using foam, work a palm sized amount of the foam in circular strokes starting at feet.

Use the residue of product that remains on the palms of your hands to elbows, knees, and feet. You only need a small amount for these areas since they absorb color more readily.

Don't wear deodorant, perfume, makeup or jewelry until the tan is finished developing.

Moisturize twice daily for a longer lasting and richer tan.

Insider Tip

To avoid streaks, look for the ingredient erythrulose in self tanners.
Wait 20 to 30 minutes before getting dressed. This is a good time to lift weights, do a pedicure, or meditate

Intimate Emergencies

Cold Sores

Catch the warning signs of an oncoming cold sore. A tingling sensation starts about 12 hours before the sore appears. Dab a little Pepto Bismol on the sore. Just the way it fights the virus that causes diarrhea it also combats a cold sore.

Sunburn

A bottle of vinegar added to a warm bath will soothe a sunburn while making skin extra soft. Try raspberry vinegar for an aromatherapy touch.

Shaving Rash

To soothe shaving irritation, chill wet chamomile tea bags and place them on the inflamed skin. Chamomile has anti-inflammatory antibacterial and pain relieving properties.

Bruises

Speed the healing with vitamin K or arnica, a homeopathic plant remedy for black and blue marks. Combine them by purchasing vitamin K in liquid form and mixing with arnica cream.

Thigh Pimples

The friction of thighs rubbing together, wearing tight pants, and panty hose all contribute to little red bumps which resemble a bad case of acne. Besides showering immediately following a workout, and wearing cotton, treat these breakouts just as you would the acne on your face. Make them less painful and allow them to heal by applying cornstarch or medicated powder to the area.

Bikini Rash

Very close shaving can make hairs split and loop under the surface of the skin. They push against your skin and cause inflammation and redness. Treat the area with tea tree oil, available at most drugstores or health stores.

Heat Rash

At the first sign, use a medicated healing lotion.
Avoid wearing friction causing tight clothing.
Keep the area that may be exposed to friction cool and dry with medicated powder.
Wear cotton clothing to allow the sin to breathe.

Bloating

Eating food too fast, talking while eating, drinking too many carbonated beverages and chewing gum can all cause bloating. They bring extra air into the intestines. When this happens you feel like you have a spare tire around your middle or you've gained five pounds overnight. You can prevent bloating by taking smaller bites and chewing your foods thoroughly. Avoid drinks that are too cold or too hot. Help relieve the bloating by drinking lemon balm tea.

Foot Odor

Just like the rest of your body, your feet perspire. The warmth and moisture of your shoes and sneakers allow odors to quickly build up.

Rub on alcohol or tea tree oil daily to kill bacteria.
Dust feet with baking soda before shoes and socks.
Avoid shoes made of vinyl which trap perspiration.
Spray antiperspirant into your shoes five minutes before wearing.

Anti-Intimacy Foods

Avoid gas producing foods, especially beans and cabbage at least 24 hours before that special event or rendezvous.

That's how long these foods can take to go through your system. Also avoid carbonated beverages, raw vegetables, and curry.

Chapter 10
Emergency Beauty

How do you solve a beauty emergency? As quickly as possible! There are some surprisingly unconventional tricks from inside the industry. They have been used forever behind the scenes because they work! When there is a beauty emergency, anything and everything will be tried. Time is big money on those sets.

Tired Skin

Revive dull skin and put on an instant glow with Alka Seltzer. It contains aspirin to soothe irritation, and the fizziness restores a healthy flush. Drop two tablets in a sink fill with cold water. Splash face several times and pat dry.

Keep Lipstick from Wandering

To keep lipstick off the glass and on your lips discreetly lick the rim of your glass before taking a sip.

Emergency Makeup Removers

1. Swipe contact lens solution over eyes with a cloth or eye pad.
2. Use fragrance-free baby wipes. Because they're made for a baby, they're gentle on your skin. They're also gentle on your budget, costing $4.00 for 80 compared to $15.00 for 30 of some of the high-end towelettes.
3. Apply castor oil with your finger.
4. Use a small amount of olive oil gently applied with a cotton ball.

Make Up Substitutes

No Eye Shadow

Use cream blush. Apply it with your fingers. Stay with bronze toned blushes, not red or pink which will make your eyes appear bloodshot.

No Lipstick

Add a small dab of petroleum jelly to powder blush. Apply with fingers.

Caked Foundation

If you find that your foundation is looking too pasty or thick, don't remove it. You can fix it in a flash!

1. Take a tissue and separate it. Gently take each piece and blot over the excess.
2. Spray your face lightly with water. Use a makeup sponge to blend.
3. Wet a thin wash cloth. Wring it as dry as possible. Carefully blot.

Clumpy Eye shadow

Blend and lift off excess with a cotton swab dipped in powder.

Creased Eye Shadow

Pick up the excess by swiping a cotton swab over the crease. Pat a little loose powder into the area with your finger to smooth and absorb shine.

Clumped Mascara

1. Dip a cotton swab in makeup remover and squeeze until almost dry. Go over lashes with the swab to remove clumping.
2. Comb lashes while they're damp with a folded tissue placed under the lash. Use a lash comb or a child's toothbrush to coax the clumps out.

Insider Tip

Prevent clumped mascara by wiping off your mascara wand before use. The end should have almost no mascara on it.

Lipstick Gone Dark

For lipstick that has gone on or stained too dark, bring down the intensity with a pale pink lipstick. First apply, rub lips together, and then wipe off excess with a tissue.

Lighten lipstick quickly with translucent loose powder. Use a very small amount.

Out of Eyeliner

Waterproof mascara is a great liquid liner that is also smudge proof.

Just dip a thin brush and swipe across upper lid.

Add a small amount of eye redness reliever to powder eye shadow and line with an angled brush.

Tired Eyes

Not enough sleep is not a fatal beauty blunder.

1. Dot concealer on the inner corner of each eye.
2. Blend shimmer cream under eye along lash line.
3. Line inside quarter of upper and lower eye lid with white eye pencil.
4. Soak two cotton balls in witch hazel and apply them to closed eyes for about a minute to refresh.

Cover Up a Cold

A raw red nose and swollen eyes with a pale drawn face is a beauty emergency to the max.

1. Pat on cream concealer and set with powder.
2. Use a peach blush stick to simulate healthy cheeks.

Disguise a Tattoo

Whether you're a model or just want to temporarily hide a tattoo, it can be done.

You will need three concealers. The first should be a yellow based medical concealer like Derma blend, the second should be one shade lighter than your skin tone. The third concealer is two to three shades lighter than skin tone.

Using a flat brush, apply the yellow based concealer over the tattoo. Be careful to apply only on the tattoo, not on the surrounding area. Then apply the one shade lighter concealer. Powder lightly over this. Finally apply the two shades lighter concealer to the tattoo. Set it with powder.

Stop a Shaving Cut

Put pressure on the cut for five minutes with a tissue soaked in a nasal decongestant spray (like Afrin).
This stops blood flow by constricting blood vessels.

Chapped, Flaky Lips

Chill a black tea bag for a couple of minutes.
Rub on clean dry lips in a circular motion.
Black tea contains tannins that exfoliate dead cells.
Follow with a lip balm or lip moisturizer.

Disguise Rosacea

Dab the reddened area with maple syrup, an anti-inflammatory that calms and soothes skin.
Rinse after two minutes.
Press undiluted dandruff shampoo on the area with a cotton ball and leave on for a minute.
Rinse with cool water.

Emergency Cuts and Cracks Solution

For those pesky cuts from shaving or the elements rely on this crazy insider tip. Use Krazy Glue! Hospitals use a similar material to stop bleeding. Dab on a drop and then immediately remove any excess.

Sore Feet

Here's an instant cure for sore tired feet. Massage your soles by running them over a cold soda can.

Remove Nail Polish Residue

To quickly get rid of staining left by bright nail polish, dissolve two denture tablets in one cup of warm water. Soak nails until the residue wipes off.

No Nail File

Use the striking strip of a matchbook as an emergency nail file.

Emergency Manicure

Rub olive oil on your nails when you need to make your nails presentable in a hurry. The olive oil will give your nails smoothness and shine, and will soften torn and damaged cuticles while softening hands.

Discolored Nails

Use whitening toothpaste on yellowed areas.

Save Dried Out Nail Polish

You can use that last bit of dried out nail polish by adding a drop of nail polish remover and shaking it. Because it is a remover, it will thin out the polish to bring it back to life.

Broken Nail

Clean off the broken nail so you can see what needs to be fixed.
Trim only enough of the nail to remove the split.
If the nail bed is split, tear off a small piece of tea bag paper.
Dab the crack with super glue and place tea bag paper on top.
Allow it to dry, and then buff the break with a nail buffer.

Insider Tip

Disguise chipped nails with magic marker if you've run out of nail polish.

Emergency Shoe or Handbag Shine

To quickly get some shine on your leather shoes, belts, etc., rub with the inside of a banana peel. Then buff off the excess with a soft cloth.

Removing Makeup Stains

Lift stains with a clean makeup sponge. Use it dry to pick up any wetness, then rinse out sponge and add soap. Blot on the stain until it's gone.

Spit That Stain Away

The enzymes in saliva break down protein based food stains. In a pinch, rub in the saliva in private, of course!

Fragrance Overload

Swab the skin with an alcohol soaked pad. Then smooth on unscented lotion to remoisturize and further diffuse the scent.

Hair Emergencies

Repair a Home Haircut

I know sometimes it's so tempting to cut that stray hair or chop a bit at your bangs that you just can't help yourself. Those bangs were in your eyes!

1. If you can, get to your stylist and have her give you a quick dry snip. It won't cost you much, and no, you're not the first.
2. Use styling gel (the stiffest you can find).
3. Get very creative with barrettes or a scarf.

Hair Static

Run a fabric softener sheet over the hair shaft to quickly tame it down.

Hair Knot

Constrain yourself from trying to brush out that knot. It will only make it worse. Instead, apply some conditioner or detangler over the tangled area to soften. Then use a bobby pin to gently pick strands out of the snag one at a time.

Never use water because although it initially makes hair more pliable will cause the knot to tighten as it dries.

Hair Frizz
Lip balm can smooth hair frizz in a pinch.

No Hair Rollers?
Use metal cans or sturdy plastic cups sized according to the volume and curl you need.

Emergency Hair Shine
Grab some vegetable oil from the kitchen (olive oil is best) and rub it in the palms of your hands to create heat, and then gently pat over hair shaft. Be sure to avoid the scalp area.

Gum in Hair!
Freeze that gum out with an ice cube. Place the cube over the gum.
Once it's stiff, the gum peels off.

Hair Indentations
Wearing clips and elastics can cause hair to have visible denting. To remove, spray hair with water and comb the dent out while blow drying on a high setting.

Remove Excess Hair Product
Sprinkle baking soda in your hair and leaning over from your waist, brush it all out.
A handful of oatmeal can be used to absorb excess grease and product. Rub the flakes into your hair and then brush them on to a newspaper.
Add volume to the roots by lifting your hair in sections and blow dry using only your fingers.

Unsightly Hair Roots
When your hair growth is really noticeable, only use a product that can be washed out.
My favorite is to take powdered eye shadow matching the color as closely as possible.
Simply rub it in with your index finger.
Yellows, gold, and peach are obvious choices for blondes.
There are lots of brown shadows to choose from for dark hair.

Hair Dye Dilemma

Tone down a garish hair disaster by massaging in a few drops of olive oil into dry hair and covering it with a shower cap for 20 minutes. Shampoo thoroughly with a clarifying shampoo or a mild dishwashing detergent.

Chin Hair

They're more likely to be coarse, and kind of stick out, and are the result of hormones. They usually happen to women who are on birth control pills, pregnant, or menopausal. If there's just a couple, pluck them.
More than a few? Consider laser or electrolysis.

Pop That Zit

Yes, there is an emergency procedure for a big pimple that threatens to ruin your day or night or life (or so it may seem).
1. Hold a very warm wash cloth against the area for a few minutes.
2. Wrap each index finger in a tissue and place them on each side of the blemish.
3. Exert pressure down then up and gently push out the clog.
4. Clean the zit out with a small amount of lemon mixed with a drop of water to tighten the pore.
5. Finish by applying eye redness reliever on a cotton swab. Hold on to the redness for about a minute.

Sleepy Eyes

To make eyes look wide awake, trace above eye liner with white, silver, or gold pencil. You can also substitute highlighter. Apply it with an eyeliner brush.

Apply beige powder or highlighter under the brows.

Puffy Eyes

Gently "piano tap" the area under the eye area to take away the puffiness from under the eye and to aid circulation.

Eye Bags

Run two metal teaspoons under very cold water. Hold on puffy area for about two minutes. Finish by applying hemorrhoid cream to the area.

The active ingredient in most hemorrhoid creams, benzocaine, causes blood vessels to contract, which reduces puffiness. Apply concealer over area.

Insider Tip

When you can't find your eyelash curler, take a metal spoon and heat it for a few seconds with a blow dryer. Press the round side of the spoon to the lashes to lift them and give them shape.

Toe Hair

Let me share a story with you that just proves how those minor details that sometimes go over looked can play a major part of the total package. I was in a salon having my nails done when this very chic and elegant woman walked in and sat down to get her pedicure. The technician that was working on her blanched as she began to place the client's feet in to the foot bath. She gently informed "Ms. Chic" that she really needed to have her large patches of toe hair waxed if she wanted to benefit from the pedicure. I was so embarrassed for this poor woman. The technician was much too loud and the poor woman was totally aghast! She most likely could not see the toe hair because she never looked at her feet with glasses! Or it never occurred to her to look that closely at her pedicure. So right now, take your contacts or glasses and look down at your feet. If you have toe hair I strongly advise you to get rid of it. Your pedicure is just is not going to look fashionable with toe hair.

1. Use a home waxing kit.
2. Shave it off each time you shave your legs.
3. If you have just a few, tweeze them out. They will grow out slowly.

Nipple Hair

Tweeze it if there's just one or two.

Consider electrolysis.

If there is a patch of hair, check out your laser options.

Nails

Nail Fungus

This is nasty, and can be spread at nail salons. Always try to bring your own instruments to prevent this and other problems. Clean them with alcohol in between visits.

To cure nail fungus, cut the nail down as far as possible so that the fungus and yeast stop growing. Spray the area with Lamisil, an anti fungal treatment available at drugstores.

Green Nail

If you have a greenish black spot on your nail, this is a bacterium, not a fungus.
To get rid of it, cut the nail down as much as possible. Rub a cotton ball soaked in a half teaspoon of bleach mixed with three teaspoons water.
If the discoloration remains after two weeks definitely see a doctor.

Butt Acne

Yes, they're embarrassing, but if you're wearing a revealing swimsuit check a three-way mirror before heading out.
Although they look like pimples, they're not. Heat, sweating, and friction are the likely culprits.
Rub benzyl peroxide infused into just enough moisturizer to create a soft paste. Use it at night, and be sure to cover the area with a gauze pad to keep the paste intact on the area.
In the morning rub it off with an acne pad.

Foot Cramp

To stop a foot cramp, press on the top of the foot between the bones that run into your big toe and second toe with your index and middle fingers.
Rub in a circular motion for about a minute. This is an acupuncture technique that will release pain relieving endorphins.

Clothing Dilemmas

No Iron

Wet the garment with a damp cloth and press on the wrinkles for a few seconds.
Using your hair dryer, gently blow dry the area and wrinkles away.
Use your flat iron to press away wrinkles.

Lint Remover

Use tape or a sticky label to remove lint. A large mailer tape if it's available. If you work in an office you've probably relied on this trick more than once.

Stain Removal

Keep a box of colored chalk on hand for stain emergencies. You can match the color of the stain with the color of the chalk, plus chalk washes right out and won't ruin fabrics like so many chemical removers can.

Bent Sunglasses

To get sunglasses that may have twisted out of shape back into service, use a hair dryer to mold the plastic.

Tight Pants Solutions

Grab an Elastic

Take an elastic band and wrap it around your button. Hook it through the button hole and then back on the button or snap.

Button Extender

Sold at fabric stores, it will give you an extra inch of room in your waist. It fits in the button hole of your pants, and then attaches to the button.

Stuck Zipper

Don't yank and break that zipper! First try these emergency insider fixes.

1. Run lip balm along the length of the zipper until it comes free.
2. Take a birthday candle, and wipe it down the zipper.

Dropped Compact

Don't cry over a smashed powder compact
Arrange the pieces back into the tin the best you can and crush them up a bit.
Add a small amount of rubbing alcohol and gently work up a paste.
Smooth it out, let it dry and it should re-form so that it's perfectly usable.

No Deodorant

If you should find yourself in the position of being out of deodorant (and need it) just make your own.
Mix together one teaspoon cornstarch with two tablespoons of baking soda.
Apply it with a powder puff or thin washcloth.

The cornstarch acts as an anti-perspirant, keeping you dry.
The baking soda will keep you smelling sweet!

Hanger Bumps

Wet the affected area with warm water.
Holding the item in one hand, apply a hair dryer set on high over the fabric.
Keep the dryer moving so that the bumps get flat but not scorched.

The heat will soften the warped fibers so that the fabric settles back into its original shape.

Chapter 11
Insider Style

Fashion is One Thing While Style is Quite Another

What is style? What is fashion? They've never been the same. Fashion changes from year to year, and season to season. It comes in quickly and disappears at a whim. Style is developed and if done well, is indelible to the wearer and remains forever.

Style Starts with Quality

Fine workmanship has nothing to do with price. No matter how it looks or fits, quality is at the forefront of a stylish look.

1. The fabric should have a good "hand".
2. Seams should be generous, stitched smoothly with finished edges, and should not pucker or pull.
3. Buttons should be functional and properly attached.
4. Buttonholes are well finished and large enough for the button to go through without pulling.
5. Hems should be invisible.
6. Sleeves should fall straight from the shoulder to wrist.
7. Linings should be an inch above the hem and straight hemmed, and should never interfere with the garment's drape.
8. Collars should fold correctly and with ease. You should not be able to detect seaming or cutting.
9. Patterns should line up and match.
10. Zippers look best dyed to match fabric and concealed.

Insider Tip

When you find a look that works for you, do what insiders do and adopt uniform dressing. This is a common thread that should run through your wardrobe. It can be that theme or signature color, cut, or garment. Change it up with different accessories, textures, and variations on that style. The good news? You'll use more of your wardrobe than most people do which is only 20 per cent.

Trend Styling

Every insider wardrobe is based on essentials. They are the key items that carry you through the day and create a working wardrobe. Once you have these basics you can take your looks to another level by mixing things up with a sprinkling of current trends. A sprinkling means just that, not a big helping of whatever is hot. It's an acknowledgement that you are up on what's happening and open to new looks, but not about to be overwhelmed by the latest and greatest. You take what you like, wear it in any way that suits you, and you look current and in control.

If you just don't feel comfortable in a new trend, then don't buy it, no matter how popular it is and what celebrity is wearing it.
Use your intuition when you shop. It will never let you down. What good are those low rise jeans if you're constantly pulling at them because they keep riding down? Your emotions and comfort always show up on your face.

Runway to Reality

It's so much fun to watch the runway shows and peruse the editorial pages of the leading magazines, but realize that what you are seeing is highly exaggerated. Obviously you're not going to go around in a sheer blouse. That's pretty obvious (I hope!). But you also cannot possibly wear five layers and why would you possibly want to? That said, one or two layers in coordinating colors can create a lovely flow of fabric while appearing creatively put together. Too many layers and you not only look like a mummy, but you lose your ability to move. The point is to take what you see in the magazines and on the runway and fit it to your own lifestyle and age.

Tales from the Runway

Buyers who come to the runway shows rarely purchase items for their stores exactly as shown on the runway. The major department store buyer will order what was shown as a very mini skirt and insist the designer tack on three additional inches. These buyers are astutely aware that their customer will not make that purchase otherwise. That gorgeous plunging blouse may be ordered, but only with the addition of a few more buttons.

Styling for a Better Body

The first rule is to buy clothing that fits you. No matter what your size, if you wear the wrong size you'll end up looking bigger than you are. Wearing clothing that is too tight adds bulges and lumps. Clothing that is too big just adds size to your body.

Choose clothing that skims over the areas you want to disguise.

Only one baggy item is allowed on your body at one time! It does not fool anyone to cloak yourself in material. Tighten up where your body is slimmest. If your upper body is slimmer, then go for a fitted top. Good legs? A great skirt or jeans will look "killer" with a longer, looser top. The eye will go right to the good stuff!

Longer pants give the look of leaner legs. You've seen it on the Red Carpet, pants so long that they are practically hitting the floor. It's a way that those Insider Beauties make their legs look miles long. Here's how you can create the look.

Choose boot cut pants and pair them with heels that should be at least half covered with the pant while standing. Be careful with the shoe or boot that you select. A stiletto could get caught in the pant. Choose a stacked heel.

All right, we've all seen those oh so embarrassing "Mom Jeans" on Saturday Night Live, but there's always a grain of truth in those parodies. No matter your size always go for a pant or jean waistband that falls below your natural waistline. It visually shrinks your hips and is much more flattering.

A little bit of stretch goes a long way in flattering the body. It flows with the body, caressing it, rather than pinching it.
The right stretch will retain it's memory and snap back into place so it never looks droopy or stretched out.

Balance is Key

Wear a fitted skirt with a frilly blouse.

Offset a full skirt with a tailored top to keep the look from going over the top.

Narrow pants require coordination with volume like a boxy jacket or a dolman top.

Slimming Style

Avoid

Cropped or wide leg pants which shorten legs

Layers of material that add volume

Horizontal details that accent wider body parts

Empire waisted dresses hide a thick waistline

Tight skirts in a light color

Tapered cuts

Look For

V-neck to slim and lengthen your torso

Details at your best body part

Classic trouser without too much volume or detailing

Styling Taller

Avoid

Long skirts with too much fabric

Long shapeless dress

Baggy pants

Look For

Above the knee skirt gives the appearance of height by lengthening the leg.

Fitted city shorts

Platform shoes. Not too retro, but with a slight lift on the toe box

Slim pants

Styling Taller (cont)

Cropped jacket
Fitted waist defining dress
Higher waist
One color or coordinating tones
Skinny anything if it can be pulled off
Body appropriate detailing

Minimize a Tummy

Use clothing that draws attention to the upper body or legs. Look for dresses that create a line from the shoulders to the middle of the leg. Tunic tops, square shaped jackets, and flat front pants are also flattering.

Get Support

Wearing the right underwear is key to looking thinner in your clothing. Thongs and g-strings are only for the very young who have no fat on their body and no sag.

Insiders know that it takes a lot of support on the inside to get perfection on the outside. So they choose the right bra. To create great cleavage, there is nothing better than a bra with criss-cross straps. It pulls the breast up and together for instant cleavage.

Look More Voluptuous

Apply blush a shade darker than your skin tone between your breasts to create cleavage and shadows. A touch of shimmer on top of each breast will highlight the breasts and make them appear fuller.

Insider's Favorite Shaper

Even though there are several shaper brands, insiders rely on long line tights because they are seamless and go all the way up to the bra line. You can replicate the effect with control top panty hose that is one size too long and has extra firm control. Hike it up under your bra for a sleek slim shape.

Minimize a Large Bust

Wear supportive bras made with quality material.

Keep away from pockets and other features that only draw attention to your breasts.

Choose open collar and v-neck tops that break up the line from your shoulder to chest.

Draw attention away from your chest with large earrings.

Style for Your Age

Twenties are a time to have fun with style. Mix up your pieces, and wear clothing that flirts.

Thirties pushes to a more fashion forward look with a figure revealing approach.

Forties style shows more femininity and accents assets. Are your arms toned? Go sleeveless. Shapely legs deserve their showcase in shorter skirts, and a deep v-neck shows off good cleavage.

Fifties becomes more sophisticated. It's sexy in an understated style. Wear jackets that fit perfectly.

Sixties are the years for polished and elegant. Careful matching and coordinating.

Seventies and Eighties call for refined definition and simplicity.

Nineties and Up? Wear whatever you want!

Rich Style

There are tricks to looking like you've got the bucks to burn. The good news is that it doesn't require a large bank account, just careful attention to the details.

Hands & Feet

Always polished, nails are never too long. Choose soft colors.

No decals or other nail art

Hair

Great color, perfect blowout and lots of shine

Skin

Not too powdered, a little shine and neutral shades in makeup with the exception of red lipstick. It looks like you spent minimal time getting ready.

Monochromatic dressing

Head to toe in one color no matter what your budget always looks pulled together.

Style with Color

Let me tell you this up front. I have never believed that certain complexions and hair color are confined to wearing only certain shades. I've never dressed my clients this way, and every insider I have worked with has never adhered to this outdated way of dressing. That said, there are certain colors which can create a mood or expression.

Green gives a feeling of freshness and balance.

Lavender is a spiritual color and gives the wearer a look of peace and serenity.

Red looks powerful and renders the wearer in control.

Pink is a highly feminine look and gives off the appearance of health and romance.

Blue is a calming color and makes the wearer look happy.

Style with White

Although white is now an option for year round wear, in order for it to work, and not come off looking like a nurse's uniform, there are considerations.

1. When wearing a white coordinate, it's important to offset the white with a bright color. White just won't work paired with a pastel.
2. White looks best ironed and crisp.
3. Cinch oversized white, or you could look like you're wearing a tent or sheet.
4. Pair white with chunky heels so the look doesn't come off too prim, or look like you're wearing a nightie.
5. Offset white with glowing skin or bright lips. Without it you'll appear washed out.

Metallics

Wearing metallic is a great way to present flair but needs to be done in moderation. Insiders use metallics with casual wear like jeans or a casual cardigan. It tends to look garish when it's overdone. You need to choose whether you will use metallic in your clothing or your accessories. You can't do both.

Metallic shines, so place it on the area that you want to highlight.

Insider Tip

A smoky eye and tousled hair works best with this look.

Going Bo Ho

Bohemian styling is often seen on insiders. One piece is all you need. Anything more is overkill. Wear a handcrafted dress with a pump. Pair a poncho with tailored jeans. Large handcrafted jewelry is best showcased on simple lines.
Peasant blouses only work when anchored with a slim line like a pencil skirt or straight pants.

Styling in the Cold

How do the insiders dress fashionably when it's freezing outside without looking like a wrapped up Eskimo? The trick is in layering.

Undergarments

Create a foundation with the right lingerie. Silk camisoles are warm and lightweight. Silk and wool socks keep feet fashionably cozy.

Legs

Switch from nylon hose to silk opaque tights. It provides fresh panache to any outfit, and looks cold weather ready.

Footwear

Choose leather or suede for wearability in wet weather. Make sure you have a rubber sole for traction in ice and snow.
Fur lined footwear is now fashionable and warming. You'll find that your feet are actually warmer when you wear this footwear without hose.

Leggings

They are warmer than hose. Replace your hose for this look.
Leggings only work when they cover a dress or skirt.

Styling for Warm Weather

When insiders dress for warm weather, they look fresh and effortless. They never look frazzled or sweaty. Here are some ways to achieve the same look.

Fabrics
Choose breathable fabrics such as cotton, linen, or rayon.

Underwear
Cotton with spandex will provide control and cool comfort.

Summer Feet
It's best to let feet breathe, so less shoe makes this possible. Sandals should not bind

Styling Footwear

The shorter the hemline, the lower the heel should be.
Wear flats with a skinny pant that ends above the ankle or cropped pants.
Shorts look best with a sandal or chunky heel. Don't even think about wearing heels with shorts.

Step up your style with bright shoes. If you don't feel brave enough to wear them with sheer or no hose, then soften the look with darker hose.

Decorative Touches
Embellishment is best added, not already attached or sewn on to a garment. You'll not only save money on your initial purchase, but you'll find that the garment will be easier to maintain and last a lot longer.

Mix and match your accessories. A brooch can add character to an otherwise drab belt. A necklace can be used as a belt or when stranded several times create a statement making bracelet.

All about Jeans

The most essential piece in your wardrobe seems so right and yet can go wrong in so many ways. The most important in choosing your jeans is fit. Be aware that you need to try on a lot of jeans before finding your most flattering fit. There is a jean out there for you. The big mistake is purchasing jeans that are too big. Most jeans stretch as you wear them so make sure that they are a little snug. Test them out by sitting down on a chair to be sure that there is no gap in the waistband.

1. Get them as long as possible without being a hazard.
2. Darker jeans look richer and make you look slimmer.
3. Purchase the heaviest weight to disguise figure flaws.
4. If you're looking to minimize your behind, choose a jean with a wider leg and a slight flare or boot cut. Avoid small or flap pockets, or embellishment that brings too much attention to the area.
5. Five pocket jeans are best for wide hips.
6. If you've got tummy issues, choose a slightly low rise jean. The jean should hit right across the tummy, not above or below it. Avoid very low rise jeans.
7. Petite bodies should choose darker jeans to elongate the leg, and a low rise.
8. Straight cut jeans are best for tall women.
9. Wide leg jeans work well on athletic builds.
10. Enhance a flat butt with slightly higher back pockets or pockets with embellishment or embroidery.

What's Never Styling

These are the looks that will not work no matter who wears them.

Elastic waists unless it's for exercising. If you must wear an elastic waist, it should always be covered.

Messages on your clothing. This includes the designer's name emblazoned anywhere, your love or hate for something or someone, or your thoughts for the day.

Don't Even Think About It
Fanny Packs
Short shorts
Lingerie as clothing
Pajamas as outerwear
Mesh unless it's an accessory
Tie Dye
Madras

Visible underwear. This includes your bra showing under a sheer blouse, panty lines, or thongs (especially thongs).

Too much sheer. Leave them guessing. Sheer arms are fine, but a sheer midriff is not.

Leggings are not pants. They only work when worn as hosiery.

Oh no you don't!

Pregnancy Style

This special time is a wonderful opportunity for creative styling, but also a real challenge to an expanding body. Insider beauties embrace their pregnancy as a way to show off their new bodies. They are no longer trying to hide themselves away.

Work with Your Current Wardrobe
During the first months of your pregnancy, you can get away with some of your regular wardrobe, even your pants. Just use the insider elastic trick to allow for waist expansion.

Loop a rubber band around the button or snap.
Thread the elastic through the button hole and then back on the button or snap.
Use larger rubber bands as you grow!

Materials Matter
Knits work because they expand as you do, retain their shape.
Spandex is an insider favorite because it shows that you are pregnant and not just gaining weight.
Solids and neutrals carry you further in your wardrobe.

Insider Tip
Accessories are fabulous when used to bring attention away from your belly. Great necklaces and earrings along with colorful scarves will add personality to everything you wear throughout your pregnancy. Stay away from bracelets and belts. Your intent is to create balance to your body.

Chapter 12
Insider Age Defying

How We Age

When it comes to aging many are lead to believe that it's either great genes or the slice of the costly surgeon's knife. There are so many alternatives that are logical and inexpensive.

Aging Criteria

Of course we all know that avoiding sun, alcohol, and smoking are age detractors. However there is something worse.

A group of over a thousand women were studied at the St. Thomas Hospital in London, England and it was found that obese women had over eight years of advanced aging. Women who smoked had over four years of accelerated aging.

It's a Daily Decision

What you do each day can add or take away your looks.
How you think greatly affects the aging process.

Calm Down and Take Control

Anger causes frown lines. When you're angry, you speed up your heart rate, raising your blood pressure. Learn to take deep breaths when you're stuck in traffic, in line, or otherwise annoyed. It's equally important not to keep your emotions in. There's nothing like standing up for what you believe in to get the blood flowing. Pick your battles.

Hang In

Don't give up and go into a deep depression like some women do the first time some kid calls you ma'am. Don't you remember when you saw someone who had let it all go, and you wondered why? Don't become a "why".

Keep Changing

Get out of the rut and change it up. You may think that your look is just fine, but change something for a day.

You can always go back if it doesn't work. Test it out and see if anyone notices.

Keep It Real

If the skin on your arms is hanging down, don't wear sleeves shirts until you can do something about them. Why do that to yourself? That said, if your legs are still great, keep on wearing those short skirts. Again, just be reasonable and reconsider short just above the knee and not short as in those psychedelic years.

Don't Play It Too Safe

Some women believe as they age, they need to become invisible. Of course you never want to become a caricature of your former self. But you don't want to fade into the woodwork. That's even more aging. Look, if you don't want to bring attention to your crow's feet, then emphasize your eyebrows.

Insider Tip

Every aging insider beauty I know meditates in some way. Scientists have found that meditation helps keep wrinkles at bay while keeping the body healthy.

A Better Body

You can virtually eat away the years, and you'll be happy to know that it's much more effective and less costly than plastic surgery or exotic creams. Insider aging beauties make their calories mean something because they know that what they eat they'll eventually end up wearing.

Strength Training

When you train for strength you'll give your muscles more shape while keeping skin tighter. It will also help relieve arthritic symptoms, increase bone density, improve posture, prevent lower back pain, and help raise metabolic rate. Free weights are inexpensive and convenient to use. Start with five pound weights and try to work up to ten pound weights. You can even make your own weights by filling a two liter bottle of soda with sand or salt.

Ageless Eating

1. Change your afternoon break from coffee to green or black tea to ward off wrinkle causing free radials.
2. Add turmeric to your salads. This spice carries anti-inflammatory properties.
3. Instead of sugar, add cinnamon to yogurt, apples, etc. Cinnamon boosts circulation.
4. Eat less food more often. If you skip meals, you're more likely to gain more weight than people who ate exactly the same amount of calories distributed evenly among more frequent meals.

Cooking

Cook in olive oil, a monosaturated fat that nourishes and protects skin's underlying support structures.
Add bulk to your cooking with low calorie vegetables rich in fiber. You'll feel more satisfied with less calories.

Insider Age Defying Foods

Asparagus
Each serving provides folic acid and other age fighting nutrients.

Beets
Full of antioxidants for the skin and detoxifiers that target the liver.

Blueberries
Contain more antioxidants than any other fruit or vegetable. Researchers have found that just one cup of blueberries daily (especially wild blueberries), quadruples anti-aging compounds that can keep wrinkles away. Tufts University conducted a study in which old rats regained youthful characteristics after being fed a diet high in blueberries.

Citrus Fruits

Packed with vitamin C to help bolster the immune system, vitamin C has been linked to smoother skin and reduced risk of arthritis.

Cherries

Contain quercetin, a powerful antioxidant that fights inflammation.

Cranberries

Contain polyphenols, full of large anti inflammatory properties. Try to include up to a cup a day.

Garlic

Cleanses pores from the inside out, lowers blood pressure, reduces cholesterol, and contains anti-bacterial antifungal properties.

Kale/Spinach

The super antioxidant leutin helps to protect eye sight and skin aging.
One to two cups a day is recommended for best results.

Kiwi

This delicious fruit contains the most vitamin C of any fruit, essential for smooth flawless skin.

Red Wine

The good news is that red wine stabilizes blood glucose levels to make cells healthier overall. The antioxidant resveratrol is the hero ingredient to aid overall health.
Drink no more than one to two glasses a day. More than that, and the benefits will be outweighed by the dangers (like liver damage).

Romaine Lettuce

Contains twice as much folic acid, six times more vitamin C, and eight times more beta-carotene than iceberg lettuce.

Sweet Potatoes

The beta carotene in model Christie Brinkley's favorite snack can combat wrinkles and help with vision.

Bake several and keep them in the refrigerator. Microwave them and sprinkle with cinnamon for a sweet age defying treat.

Tomatoes

Nature's number one source of lycopene, an antioxidant that fights tissue damaging free radicals.

Yogurt

Full of calcium and one of nature's oldest health foods to fight high blood pressure. Most beneficial when thickened with live cultures rather than gelatin.

Age Defying Hair

Reverse the Strands of Time

Your hair ages along with everything else. The hair shaft begins to lose volume and becomes more fragile and drier.

Hormonal changes will cause hair strands to gray. You'll find that your hair will also begin to feel much coarser.

Calcium is beginning to build up in the follicle restricting the growth of hair to the shaft. The growth cycle is changing, and more follicles are now resting.

Choices

There's a lot that can be done. A new and refreshing hair color, a more flattering cut, and some simple restorative techniques can make a huge difference.

Loosen your hair. Tight hair or "helmet hair" looks dated and ages you. Plus it looks like you don't know how to care for your hair. Stiff hair no matter how it's styled looks old. Solve this problem and take away the years by limiting or eliminating hair spray.

Make It Shine

Shine is young and matte is old especially with aging hair. There are many effective shine-enhancing treatments and glosses on the market. Your stylist can give you a professional shine treatment.

Insider Tip

A wash-in hair gloss can enhance your natural color or you can purchase a tinted color to easily hide gray.

Gray Games

Some women become even more fabulous by embracing their gray while others are relieved that they can experiment with coloring and not have to worry about the frequent touch ups of their darker days. Some women look great, while others can appear washed out when going gray.

Don't use high heat on gray hair as it will singe and turn yellow and brassy.
Don't overuse relaxers. Gray tends to make straightened hair look even more coarse.
Be careful using colored gels and styling products. Gray hair absorbs hair more quickly.

Almost Natural

If your hair is less than half gray, you probably can get away with a semi-permanent color. Choose one with no ammonia. You'll find that not only does a semi-permanent color cover the gray, but will boost shine while looking very natural.

Choose Your Favorite Length

Insider beauties don't let age define their length. They don't chop off their hair just because they've reached a landmark birthday. Some women look great in short hair while some cannot carry it off no matter what their age.
However, hair past the shoulders does drag the face down.
Layers are youthful on all lengths.
Consider the youthful effects of a face framing style.

Volumizing Shampoo

Look for the ingredient polyquaternium-10 to achieve more body in your hair. This ingredient also acts as a detangler.

Age Defying Makeup Techniques

Makeup can be a beauty maker or breaker. It has the ability to make you look like a clown or years younger. But you simply can't defy age without it.

Brows

Very thin eyebrows can drag your eye down and looks dated. Eyebrows are the shoulder pads that hold up the face. Eyebrows provide a focal point that demands attention A slightly over grown brow looks better than a perfectly groomed brow, and you can give it a nice shape with brow powder and gel.

Blush

Use pink or peach blush, never brown. If you want to contour, do so with a slightly darker foundation than your regular color. Always use blush with a strong eye treatment to balance the face.
Smile as broadly as you can when applying blush.

Hooded Eyes

Drooping eyes prevent makeup from looking smudge proof and fresh looking.
Keep shadow in a light neutral shade, and contour the eye itself with liner. If you have wrinkling or puffiness below the eye, soft shadow placed right under eye can deflect and soften the area.

Brush Away Crow's Feet

Apply pale shadow over fine lines and they'll virtually disappear when the light hits them. Try to find a shimmering foundation, or you can dip a brush into a shimmery eye shadow and then into your regular foundation. "Brush" into the lines.

Insider Tip

Give yourself an instant smile lift. Paint your smile lines with concealer, and then lightly powder over.
Use an eyeliner brush for the best effect.

Foundation Changes

Slightly moisten your fingers when applying foundation. If you use a sponge, wet it slightly. A little moisture provides a dewy young surface.

Apply moisturizer, then smooth on a firming gel. Leave it on and it will smooth and tighten your skin temporarily under your foundation.

Application Advice

Tilt your head slightly when looking in the mirror and applying eye products. Don't look down into the mirror or you won't get your makeup close enough to the eye.

Sunless Face Slimming

Bronzing powder can go a long way in making your face look both slimmer and younger. The key in believable bronzing is not to try to go too dark. The color looks best when it's one or two shades darker than your natural skin tone. Just replace your regular finishing powder with the bronzer, and you can look radiant throughout the seasons.

Apply it where the sun would naturally color your face, nose, cheeks, chin, and forehead. Skip the area right under the eye. Use only enough to color. You'll know you've applied too much when it looks powdery.

Lips

The perfect lipstick can take years away from your face. It sends the attention to your lips rather than to sagging mouth wrinkles or a sagging jaw line. Be diligent in keeping to the lip line. Extending beyond will only accentuate lines.

Ageless Style

It's a style that defies rules, especially the fashion dictates of past generations. If there weren't black and white rules in the past, there were definite obligations and restrictions that sapped our adventurous spirits and creativity.

Adjust Accordingly

The body changes as it ages, but you can dress to compensate for that. Baggy clothing drags the body down and adds weight. Too-tight clothing shows every lump and bump. If you end up with red welts on your body then you need to go up a size.

Stay Solid

Prints make you look like you are your own grandma, and never flatter your body. A little print goes a long way. If you love prints, wear them away from your face. A print skirt or pants with a solid top is age defying. A print top with sequins is aging.

Ageless Skin

Menopause and Your Skin

Aging skin is prone to bruising even with just a little bump. Thinning skin and a loss of collagen is the culprit.
Use vitamin K to heal that bruise quickly.

Pimples at My Age?

Your oil glands produce less oil but it's thicker causing clogged pores. Use salicylic acid pads to unclog them. Don't use it all over the face, just in the T-zone.

Combating Rough Skin

Use vitamin A capsules in the rough patches.
Be aware that vitamin A has a tendency to peel skin.
Never apply it near the eye area.

Anti Wrinkle Mask

Mix 1 egg yolk with 1 teaspoons milk or 1 teaspoon yogurt.
Apply to freshly washed face.
Allow to set for about 10 minutes.
Rinse and follow with moisturizer.

Agers to Avoid

What worked yesterday has to be reconsidered to compensate for the changing face and body.

Frosted Nails

Frosted, taupe, or brown nails make hands look older. Choose bright colors to bring the attention to the nails and not the hands.

Dark Lipstick

Lighten up your lipstick. It's much more forgiving to the aging face. Choose sheer formulas.

Straight Hair

Fringing the hair, whether its bangs or cheek fringing softens the face. A severe style is rarely flattering.

Heavily Powdered Eye Shadow

Cream shadow softens the eye while powdered shadow accentuates every single wrinkle.

Pleated Slacks

They don't hide tummies. They are an arrow pointing directly to it.

Cowl Necklines

They just droop, and aging beauties have enough drooping to contend with.
Dropped necklines in general should be worn with jewelry or a scarf to compensate.

Aging Choices

1. Choose anti-aging serums over creams. Serums are more potent. Add a cream over the serum if necessary.

2. Squinting causes lots of wrinkles so make sure you never leave the house without sunglasses, and have your eyes checked regularly.

3. Choose one color theme in clothing and cosmetics. Too many colors are anything but youthful. They tend to look clownish.

4. Loosen up . Don't stay married to that hairstyle or favorite cosmetic. If something you love has been discontinued don't try to track it down. Move on and try something new.

Strike Oil!

Aging insider beauties rely on borage oil for fighting under eye puffiness.

It is a hormone like substance that helps ease inflammation and expel excess fluid that collects in the under eye area.

Celebrity Age Defying

Kim Basinger
The Oscar winning actress and former model is a big believer in colonic irrigation therapy. She believes that detoxifying her body keeps her skin glowing and controls her weight.

Goldie Hawn
Looking great after 60 exemplifies the lifestyle of this long time actress. Her diet is wheat-free, dairy-free, and sugar-free. Her favorite ways of staying in shape include power walking and weight training.

Angela Bassett
She's kept that rocking body she worked so hard to get to play Tina Turner. Angela lifts weights and works the treadmill while watching her favorite TV shows.

Jerry Hall
The former super model and ex wife of Mick Jagger doesn't believe she needs to cut her hair just because she's now over 50. She does believe in salt scrubs and seaweed wraps, and still uses vegetable shortening as a super rich moisturizer.

<u>Fat Blocking Soup</u>

Celebrities including Donna Karan and Ashley Judd rely on this soup to keep their weight in check.
At only 33 calories a serving, it's a sure way to get into that special event dress!

Combine 1/3 cup each chopped broccoli, zucchini, and rutabaga.
Add one chopped onion, a teaspoon of cilantro, and one cup of water.
Bring to a boil.
Cover and simmer until tender.

Makes one serving

Chapter 13
Bargain Beauty

What a Deal!

Who doesn't love a bargain? Who among us doesn't want to look as fabulous as possible without a lot of time, money, or effort? More than any insider secret coveted it's the big "I have this wonderful technique and I don't have to spend a lot" to get my results.

Bargain Skin Care

Skin care is cost effective. Take care of it, and you'll end up spending less on corrective products like concealers and clarifiers. Your skin should be your first beauty priority because it's the canvas for the rest of your looks. Your makeup no matter how advanced can't possibly look good on neglected, abused skin.

Power Up Your Rituals

After showering or bathing rub sesame or olive oil all over to seal in moisture.

Use raw sugar to exfoliate your skin. You can purchase convenient individual packets at most grocery stores. Find them in the baking aisle.

Lighten dark patches of skin on elbows, knees, and under arms with a soft paste of lemon and sugar.

Make It Last

Intensify your perfume and make it last longer by dabbing petroleum jelly on your pulse points before applying.
The perfume will adhere more easily to the jelly than it does to dry skin.

Bargain Wrinkle Peel

Here's a natural yet effective alternative to expensive chemical peels.
Mash up a green papaya and apply it directly to your skin. Let it set for 30 minutes.
Green papayas contain rejuvenating antioxidants and papain, an enzyme that dissolves damaged skin cells and promotes cell turn over.

Bargain Blemish Busters

For mild breakouts keep benzyl peroxide in your medicine cabinet, available over the counter at drugstores. It is highly effective at killing the bacteria that causes acne. Apply it with a cotton ball or cotton swab to clean dry skin. Only dab on the blemish itself, not on the surrounding area.

Apply hemorrhoid cream to a large bump about a half hour before applying makeup.

Dab Milk of Magnesia on the pimple to quickly absorb oil and disinfect. Let it dry, and then rinse off before applying makeup.

Hold an ice cube on the pimple for one minute. The ice constricts blood vessels

Cold Sores

To treat a cold sore or fever blister, take a teaspoon of baking soda and add a drop of warm water to create a paste. Apply to blister and allow to harden for about 10 to 15 minutes. The sodium bicarbonate in baking soda reduces bacteria to speed healing.

Eczema

If you suffer from eczema, evening primrose oil may be useful. It contains gamma-linolenic acid (GLA). There are skin products made with primrose oil, but a more effective and less expensive solution is to purchase the oil or individual capsules in pure form. Apply to eczema patches.

Insider Tip

Eat parsley. Homeopathic practitioners claim it keeps eczema under control.

Massage Therapist Secret

Mix together 4 tablespoons sea salt with ½ cup olive oil and the juice of one lemon. Massage the mixture over dry skin all over the body, staying away from the face and neck. Shower off under warm water with a coarse wash cloth.

Anti-Bloating Treatment

Magnesium chloride found in salt water can actually draw out excess water weight. To help with bloating due to PMS, too much salt, or simply to look fabulous in that figure revealing dress, add one cup of Epsom salts to a warm bath and soak for at least 15 to 20 minutes.

Sunburn Reliever

Mix one teaspoon of Aloe Vera gel with one teaspoon honey. Apply it to the affected area for a few minutes.

Rinse off with cool water. The mixture will cool the skin while preventing peeling.

Bargain Hair

Dandruff Treatment

To get rid of dandruff, mix equal amounts of apple cider vinegar and warm water and apply to your scalp. Gently massage in and then wrap your head in a towel for 30 minutes.

Shampoo, rinse, and condition.

How it works.

Dandruff is a type of yeast that lives on the scalp. Vinegar is acidic and destroys yeast.

Intense Conditioner

For a deep conditioning treatment head to your local health store and pick up a bottle of wheat germ oil in capsule or liquid form. Wheat germ oil will help repair fragile, broken, and weak hair. Prick open two gel capsules or apply one tablespoon to dry hair. Allow to set for 10 minutes, and then shampoo and rinse.

Oregano & Vanilla Hair Detangler

Combine two teaspoons dried oregano with one teaspoon vanilla extract and one cup water. Microwave this mixture for 30 seconds.

When cool, strain and pour into a spray bottle.

Use after shampooing and conditioning as a leave in detangler.

Keeps in refrigerator for up to a week.

Bargain Style Rules

It's the little things that can create a look that goes beyond dollars. The most inexpensive garment can look like absolutely couture when it's worn it's worn in an insider way. We all remember Sharon Stone walking the red carpet with a Gap shirt and a long skirt. Mixing high and low is an insider bargain favorite way to style.

Go Faux!

A great way to create a high end look and save a ton of money is to go faux!
Celebrities do it all the time, and you'd be surprised at how often they do. Everyone from Paris Hilton to Jennifer Lopez not only wear fakes, but they mix them in with their real gems.
To get the most expensive appeal, look for stones that are encased in four prong settings Low quality fakes are just glued in place.
A good fake will be heavy. The really cheap stones are light and flimsy.
Go smaller if you're trying to pass off your fake as real. A huge stone is a dead give away.
Plus, with a smaller stone the flaws won't be as visible.

Bargain Tools

These are the work horses of your makeup tools.

Cotton Swabs

Perfect for blending eye shadow, creating a smoky eye look, and picking up makeup smudges.

Clean Mascara Wand

Recycling has never been so convenient. Clean your old mascara wands and use them as eyebrow groomers and to separate lashes. Clean them with soap and water or makeup remover.

Sponges

Those disposable makeup sponges sold at discount and drugstores are what makeup artists use to get a precise application of foundation, to blend colors, and to clean up excess product.

Brush Break

For superior natural bristle brushes which makeup artists rely on as the best and longest lasting, skip the department stores and head to your local art supply store. There you can get the same pony, sable, and goat hair brushes in a variety of sizes at a fraction of the price. For example, a brush that can cost $30 at a cosmetic counter is only $6 to $8 at an art supply store.

Bargain Cosmetic Case

Hit the school supply section of your local drugstore or office supply store and pick up a transparent pencil pouch.

They become lightweight and sturdy cosmetics bags that make it easy to see the entire contents of the bag at a glance.

You'll save your nails, and you'll save tons of money. You can get one for less than $2.00!

Save Your Leftover Shadows

If you find yourself with eye shadows that you rarely use because they just aren't your favorite shades, don't throw them away. You can create your own unique colors. Take the eye shadows out with a spoon or small screw driver.

Place them in a pill box, and then gently break them with a small knife. Be creative and mix the shades until you find a color you like.

Insider Tip

Blend pink or peach eye shadow with a small amount of pressed powder and use it as a soft blush.

The Biggest Bargain Tool Secret

It's your fingers! Your body heat warms up your product before application, and you'll have better control.

Use your index finger to pat color onto the skin.

Apply eye cream with your pinky finger to insure minimal pressure to this delicate skin.

Bargain Shopping

The best bargain shoppers don't follow magazine dictates of purchasing as soon as the season starts. They shop mid or end of the season when the sales are just too good to resist. The trick is to concentrate on classics. If you are crazy over a trend then purchase it at a discount or mass merchandise store. Then it won't be a big deal or financial failure at the end of the season if you throw it out.

Shop Discount

Everyone does! Insider beauties get all their basics from mass merchandisers who sell everything from bras to bleach. Tee shirts from Target, Wal-Mart, and K Mart are purchases too good to pass up in classic colors. Look for 5% spandex for great fit and durability.

Insiders Love Vintage

Whether it's from EBay or an obscure thrift shop, getting something that's unique and memorable is an insider beauty trademark.

Rules for Bargain Shopping

1. Shop with an open mind. If you have your heart set on something specific then you're better off in a major department store.
2. Look for designers or brands that you know fit you well.
3. Search out things that will mix and match with other clothes that you have.
4. Stock up on items you will definitely wear season after season.
5. Concentrate on colors you know you look good in.
6. Check for stains or excess handling.
7. Choose quality fabrics and workmanship.
8. Select styles that are not garnished with too much embellishment that will outdate the garments too soon.
9. Check seams and hems for sturdiness and workmanship.
10. Keep tags on your items until you've taken inventory of your closet and coordinated your new finds with at least 3 other items.

Get the Most for Your Money

Extend the seasons of your wardrobe by layering crewnecks and tees under your warm weather items.

Classic cardigans can warm up sleeveless and short sleeve wear.

Ankle boots and closed pumps allow warm weather clothing to go into colder weather.

A funky and dollar saving option is to wear your sandals into cold weather by pairing them with opaque hose

Chapter 14
Insider Supplements

The Importance of Supplements

Insiders have found that a once a day multi vitamin is not enough. There are highly targeted supplements that can do everything from repair cells to burn fat.

Researchers have discovered that the new antioxidants can combat free radicals and repair skin cells. If used intelligently the right supplements can rejuvenate the body, restore radiance to the skin, and carries the potential to delay aging and protect key cells.

Be a Knowledgeable Consumer

Purchase your supplements from a trusted source.

All ingredients should be clearly listed. Check the expiration date. Check if there are certification stamps or programs.

Use standardized herbs. If an herb is standardized then you have some assurance that the product contains active ingredients at a set concentration.

Be very wary of using supplements or herbs if you are pregnant or nursing. Little is known about what they might do to an unborn baby. Do not give them to young children.

Be careful about mixing supplements and prescription medications since some substances can interact negatively.

Don't take any supplements at least two weeks before surgery.

Report adverse reactions. Stop taking the supplement immediately and report reactions like skin rash, headache, or stomach upset to your doctor.

Better Nails

Take a vitamin with biotin, a B vitamin proven to strengthen nails. Foods that contain biotin include peanuts, egg yolks, corn, and cauliflower.

Healthier Hair

Studies have shown that gamma linoleic acid (GLA), an omega fatty acid, is the optimum nutrient for hair. You can purchase borage seed oil, the richest source of GLA at most health food stores. The recommendation is for 500 mg twice a day.

Insider Favorite Supplements

Alpha Lipoic Acid

Vital for cell energy production, and protects against free radicals. Reduces blood sugar. It is considered one of the most powerful and beneficial anti-inflammatory antioxidants to fight aging and weight problems by aiding cellular metabolism.
Recommended dosage 500 mg

B Complex

A daily B-Complex supplement that contains folic acid has the ability to fend off gray hair and restore natural hair color
Recommend dosage 400 mcg

Coenzyme Q10

Helps in energy production and protects cells against free radicals, benefiting skin.

Chromium Picolinate

An essential mineral that helps your body use sugar better and reduces cravings by regulating insulin production.
Recommended dosage 200 to 400 mcg

Cur cumin

This supplement is a derivative of turmeric (a spice).
It helps the skin fight inflammation.
Recommended dosage 1,000 mg

DMAE

A compound naturally found in sardines and salmon. Stimulates body naturally and internally moisturizes skin.

Recommended dosage 100 to 500 mg

DHEA

Controversial yet widely used by insiders. Stimulates hormones lost during the aging process. Used as a natural hormone replacement. Touted as the fountain of youth, it is believed to benefit energy (including sexual energy), firmer skin, and thicker hair.

Recommended dosage 25 milligrams starting at age 35 until the age of 50

After 50 the dosage is recommended at 50 mg

Flax

Contains powerful anti-aging compounds. Also used for appetite suppressing qualities and proper elimination.

Recommended dosage 1 to 2 tablespoons

GLA

An essential fat, gamma linolenic acid works internally to heal and replenish skin.
Follow label directions.

Ginger

Contains compounds that have antioxidant, anti-inflammatory effects
Recommended dosage 500 mg

Glucomannan

A natural fiber pill made from a Japanese plant that reportedly reduces blood sugar levels by 28% for at least two hours if taken before eating sugary or high carbohydrate foods. It holds more water than most fiber so it makes you feel full faster and slows the absorption of glucose into the bloodstream.

Recommended dosage 1 gram 20 minutes before each meal

Grape seed

Decreases destruction of collagen and helps stabilize and strengthen cartilage of joints. Has anti aging effects.

Recommended dosage 100 to 300 mg

Green Tea

Antioxidant with metabolism enhancing qualities

Recommended dosage 3 cups or 400 mg

Horsetail

Improved skin, hair, and nails

Recommended dosage 50 mg

L-Carnitine

Enhances use of fats and increases metabolism by burning fats.

Recommended dosage 500 mg

Pregnenolone

A natural nutritional supplement that is reported to enhance mental alertness and lubricates joints. Derived from the extract of wild yam, the hormone already exists in our bodies but declines as we age. It is also reported to greatly improve resistance to stress and helps with vision, making colors brighter and clearer.

Primrose Oil

Gamma linoleic acid (GLA) an essential fatty acid found in evening primrose oil has been proven to produce gradual weight loss by firing up the metabolism.

Recommended dosage 3,000 to 6,000 mg

Pycogenol

A pine tree bark extract shown to bolster collagen and elastin, improve blood and nutrient flow to skin cells, reduce skin inflammation, and help rebuild collagen.

Psyllium

A fiber that shuts down the urge to eat and slows down the absorption of excess fats. This supplement keeps fat from sticking, and swells to nine times its size by the time it reaches the stomach.

Quercetin

Found naturally in apple skin, onions, cherries, and tea.
Studies show these antioxidants in this supplement inhibit inflammation.
Recommended dosage□500 mg

Spirulina

This blue-green algae is an anti-inflammatory which makes it beneficial to skin tone.
Add a tablespoon to yogurt or cereal, or take it as a tablet.

Chapter 15
Beauty Breakthroughs

There are new and inventive breakthroughs in appearance improvements that are both exciting and cautionary. Although I have outlined the latest techniques as well as their benefits and risks, it is important to be an informed consumer.

New Non Surgical Techniques
Permanent Lip Plumping

Lips thin out and droop as we age. There are now long term and permanent breakthroughs to consider.

Restylane

A hyaluronic acid, and a sugar based gel found naturally in rooster combs. It's given by injection to define and to add volume. It's used to raise drooping corners of the mouth, which turn down during the aging process.

Results: 6 to 12 months.

Cost: $500 to $600

Possible Complications: temporary lumps and redness

Hylaform

Similar to Restylane, also a hyaluronic acid, it is injected into the lip area to restore volume.

Results: 3 to 6 months

Cost: $400 to $500

Possible Complications: Redness

Fat Injections

Fat is removed from abdomen or hip through light liposuction and injected into the lips.

Results: Several months to permanent depending on body's reaction

Cost: $1,000 to $1,200

Possible Complications: Temporary lumpiness and redness

Porcelain Veneers

Cosmetic veneers, used to give small or irregular teeth better shape and size can also plump out the appearance of lips. It's a two for one procedure and used by many insiders. Not only do your teeth look better, but your lips will look fuller without any needles!

Results: Permanent

Lip Line Solutions

Botox

A substance produced from botulinum toxin that temporarily immobilizes the muscles under the skin. It can be injected in very small doses to reduce the lines above the lip.

Results: 4 to 6 months

Cost: $300 to $400

Possible Complications: Temporary redness and unevenness

Laser Resurfacing

There are now effective laser techniques to get rid of lip lines. It is a long term solution, and results won't appear until several weeks.

Results: 12 months or more

Cost: $1,500 to $2,000

Possible Complications: discoloration and redness

New Uses for Botox

Botox has emerged from just paralyzing wrinkles or releasing frown lines to treating almost every part of the body. Make certain that the procedure you are interested in has been approved by the Food and Drug Administration.

Lift a Droopy Nose

The right amount of Botox can give a subtle lift to a droopy nasal tip.

Stop Excess Perspiration

Botox has been used successfully to treat the palms of the hands, armpits, and feet. A few doctors are also experimenting with Botox to treat excessively oily scalps.

Fix a Gummy Smile

The muscle actions for smiling can sometimes elevate too much, causing too much gum to be shown. Botox can reduce the elevation action of your mouth and eliminate this problem.

TMJ Relief

Some doctors have begun using Botox in relieving TMJ stress and other symptoms related to TMJ.

Relax Neck Bands

When muscles are overly tight in the neck it can cause a severe look. Relaxing those muscles with Botox can smooth them out and give off a more youthful appearance.

Lift Mouth Corners

Muscles around the mouth can pull down, causing a frowning appearance.
Botox can relax these muscles, resulting in a natural looking neutral position.

Non Surgical Wrinkle Removers

Thermage

This procedure uses radio frequency technology to stimulate collagen production which results in tighter skin and fewer wrinkles. Each session takes about an hour. Although FDA approved (since 2003) there have been some cases of burning. Done properly, this procedure leaves skin with a smooth glow, tightens brows, neck, and jaw line.

Thermage is for sagging due to loss of skin tone, rather than for removing excess fat. It does not treat fat pockets.

Most Thermage procedures are done in 3 to 6 sessions.

Cost: $3,000 to $6,000.

Lasers for Wrinkling

Called Fraxel SR or Fractional Skin Resurfacing, this treatment removes the upper layers of skin.

Another technology that is even newer than Fraxel SR is Lux IR. It combines the resurfacing technology of Fraxel SR with the tightening effects of Thermage.
You'll need 2 to 3 sessions.
Cost: $1,000 to $2,000

Cellulite Slimming Sneakers

New to the market, and worn by insiders to fight cellulite, tone muscles, improve posture and balance, and also reduce the look of varicose veins.

Insiders Favorite Surgeries

Blepharoplasty

When skin starts to sag at the brow bone, this type of surgery may solve the problem. It is sometimes combined with a brow lift, especially when the eyelid skin comes down. This type of surgery is usually done endoscopically through tiny incisions, and just the outer corners of the brow are pulled back.

Arm Lift

The name for removing excess skin from drooping arms is brachioplasty. An incision is made in the arm and depending on the severity of the drooping, may continue along the inside of the arm to the elbow.
Cost: $5,000 to $6,000

Problem: Lumpy Butt

Non Surgical Solution

Vela Smooth & TriActive

Both incorporate light based energy combined with mechanical massage.
Requires a series of treatments.

Surgical Solution

1. Buttock Lift

Usually combined with a body lift. The skin and underlying matrix are separated from the muscle and fat, releasing bands that cause cellulite and lumping.

2. Subcision

This is less invasive surgery originally used for acne scars. It improves the look of cellulite by releasing the fibrous bands under the skin that cause the rippled look. The positive aspect of this procedure is that it's done under local anesthesia. There is the possibility of potential scarring, and Subcision is not without pain or bruising.

Problem: Loose Stomach Skin

Non Surgical Solution

Titan

A non invasive light based treatment which is done as a series. It usually takes two treatments which are done four weeks apart. It minimally tightens skin, but is not as effective as a tummy tuck.

Surgical Solution

Tummy Tuck

Also known as abdominoplasty, the intent is to reshape and firm the abdomen. The apron of the stomach is reduced under general anesthesia.

Approximate Costs of Surgery

Of course, the cost of surgery varies according to the surgeon in question, the area of the country where the service is provided, as well as other factors. However here are some general approximations to help you plan.

2006 National Averages

Arm Lift $6,000

Botox $300

Collagen Injection $350

Chemical Peel $3,000

Cheek Implant $2,800

Chin Augmentation $2,500

Face Lift $15,000

Liposuction $5,000

Rhinoplasty $8,000

Tummy Tuck $8,000

Breast Augmentation $6,000

Breast Reduction $6,000

Breast Implant Removal $2,500

Chapter 16
Body Beauty

Insiders employ every trick imaginable to attain and keep a great body. Here are some favorites from the bodies we all admire.

Better Body Tricks

1. **Create a Daily Menu**. Write down what you plan to eat for the day. Check off each food item as you eat it.

2. **Measure and Weigh Everything!** Estimating portions just doesn't work. We tend to be overly generous with our portions. Once you start, you'll become an expert and what seems tedious now will pay off in calories.

3. **Keep Track of Your Weight**. Even though you think you may have gained don't be afraid to get on that scale. Keeping a daily check of your progress keeps you on track.

4. **Clear Your Head**. When your brain keeps telling you that you need to binge, remove yourself from your environment. Take a walk, run errands, etc. and you'll find that the distraction will take you away from those "voices in your head" beckoning you to go off your game.

5. **Get Enough Sleep.** Get to bed early, and nap if necessary. You can fall into a dangerous "night eating" situation or find yourself eating to stay awake.

6. **Keep Pictures Around**. You'll find this to be especially helpful if you keep pictures on the refrigerator or favorite food cabinet. It may be a vacation destination, a special event you're planning to attend, or even a picture of you at your lightest or heaviest. Whatever motivates you to step away from the bad stuff.

7. **Be Aware of Your Mood.** Writing down their mood before they picked up something to eat has helped beauty insiders stay away from emotional eating traps.

8. **Cut it up**. Taking small bites helps to make a meal last longer and be more satisfying. Chow down in big mouthfuls and you'll be asking yourself, "Where did it go?"

9. **Just Say "No"!** Social eating is a scary trap. Don't avoid the social scene just because you're watching your weight. Go for the people. Become the designated conversationalist. You can hold a beverage in your hand if it makes you feel more comfortable.

10. **Always Eat breakfast**. Insiders know that this meal jump starts their metabolism and gives them energy that further burns calories.

Firm Up Your Arms

To get your arms toned and tight without getting bulky, use light free weights from 5 to 8 pounds. Research has shown that weight training is more effective for building bone strength than running or even swimming.

Improve Your Jaw line

Get rid of a double chin with this simple exercise that can be done whenever you have a spare moment.

Open your mouth and pull your lower lip over your bottom teeth.
Move your jaw up and down in a semi circular motion.
Try to do this at least 25 times a day.
This exercise works the platysma muscle and is highly effective.

Insider Butt

Flat butts are out, and firm, voluptuous behinds are all the rage! If that's the look for you, here's some ways to go.

Jeans

The right pair of jeans can do wonders for lifting and shelving a proper butt. The wrong pair can flatten you out like a pancake! There are jeans that are made to enhance any backside. Make sure you try lots of different pairs in a three way mirror. Look for name brands that advertise this feature on their tags.

Bikini

This product is known as the bra for the butt. It supports and lifts small derrieres, and lifts and rounds out large buttocks. More information is available at biniki-fashions.com.

Invisible Fanny Panty

These are high cut control briefs that add padding to the butt. Find them at Fredericks of Hollywood (fredericks.com).

Exercise

Squats can do wonders to lift and firm your butt. Holding a dumbbell in each hand speeds up the process. Lunges are fabulous for lifting and you can do them anywhere and anytime. Insider beauties do them while they're brushing their teeth, talking on the phone, or watching their favorite show.

Surgery

The Brazilian Butt Lift combined with liposuction is another option insider beauties use to achieve the perfect butt. First liposuction is used to remove fat from arms, legs, or abdomen and added to buttocks with a series of injections done six weeks apart.
For a better shaped butt, liposuction is used to reduce fat on hips and outer thighs.

Low Cost Skin Firmer

Coffee contains tannic acid that stimulates circulation and draws excess fluid from surface tissues. It's the major ingredient in many firming lotions. Dip a coarse wash cloth into a cup of warm (not hot) coffee, and massage into areas of the body that need firming and detoxing. Rinse off in the shower after allowing coffee to remain on the skin for about five minutes.

Straw Alert

There's nothing innocent about that cute little straw. Who would think that drinking from a straw could keep you from your best body? Well in the modeling industry straws are not allowed on the set ever!

Why?

The process of drinking from a straw brings air to the stomach, causing bloat and a distended middle. Experts say it also causes wrinkles.

Sipping carbonated or citrus drinks from a straw can wear away tooth enamel because of the citric and phosphoric acids. If you do use a straw, be sure to place the straw near the back of the mouth so that the acids are away from the teeth.

Limit Diet Soda

The artificial sweeteners and sodium contained in diet drinks can sabotage your quest for a better body. It seems that the body responds to all sweeteners, artificial or not, with a surge of insulin, a hormone that triggers cravings for more sweets.

Get Your Fruits and Vegetables

Concentrate on dark and deep colors.

Spinach, broccoli, kale, and green beans are highly recommended.

Watermelon, pomegranate, and dark grapes are healthy fruit choices.

Foods to Avoid

White foods like refined flour, rice, sugar, etc.

Red meat

Artificial sweeteners

Highly processed foods

Chapter 17
Beauty Occasions

Attending a special event is the perfect opportunity to showcase your ultimate style. It's now appropriate to expose more skin no matter what your age or weight, and to go that extra step without looking like you've tried too hard. It would be disrespectful not to try to look your best when you've been given that invitation.

General Rules

The idea is to take your look up a notch with added polish.
Showcase one or two special pieces of jewelry
Concentrate on rich textures in colder weather like brocades and velvet.
Warmer weather calls for lace, silk, and sheer.
These fabrics instantly present a special occasion feeling.

Go From Office to Party

Wear a small amount of makeup during the day so that when you get ready for the evening you are working on a fresher face. It is never necessary to stat from scratch unless you've been involved in a job that involves heavy physical activity.

Simple attire is perfect when you're not sure what the dress code is for the evening. Wear it with one or two pieces of special jewelry.

During the day wear a dress with a jacket or cardigan and opaque hose.
Switch to sheer or shimmery hose. Swap your flats or boots for heels.

Avoid shoes you can't walk in so practice before that event.
When in doubt stick with the basics.
Mix unexpected things like cashmere and shine.

The Right Jewelry

Wearing jewelry is an important touch to a special occasion, especially in the evening because it catches the light as you move. Brunettes look best in white gold or silver. Blonde complexions are most flattered by gold.

Earrings

Use drop earrings when hair is pulled back, but avoid them if you have a short neck.
Studs are always perfect, no matter what the occasion. Increase their size with the formality of the event.

Hair Embellishment

Instead of wearing jewelry, a special occasion is a great time to try different hair accessories. This look works perfectly when your attire is so embellished that any jewelry would be too over the top.

1. A big silk flower is a great substitute for a hat, and can dress up even the most simple hair style. Use it in a ponytail or to pull back an unruly section of hair.

2. Give your hair a party perfect finish by spritzing it with shine spray. Apply shine on dry hair and brush through for even distribution. Ceramic and ionic hair dryers and flat irons also help increase shine.

Put On a Party Face

Your regular makeup routine just won't work at night. You need to double the intensity of your cosmetics or your makeup won't show up in artificial lighting.

Use a skin luminizer to light up skin under party lights. Apply it to cheekbones, over the nose, or above blush. It also looks great on the inner eye. Apply it over foundation and powder.

Use lip gloss over your regular lipstick. It will give your lips a sultry look and catch the light. Use brighter blush and darker lipstick.

Choose a Feature

Select one area of your face to focus on when applying makeup. Dark eyes should be paired with light lips. Insiders love this look because it blends drama with innocence.

Dress Up for Candlelight

There is a technique for making up for this unique lighting. Use light pink eye shadow on the inner corner and pink shimmer cream on cheekbones and the tip of the nose. These features will become "lit" by dim candle lighting.

Insider Tip

Wear dark lipstick with big jeweled earrings. The light from the earrings will bring attention right to the lips.
It's like a neon directional sign!

Make It Last

Keep your makeup on the entire night buy spraying a brush or powder puff with a very light spritz of hairspray.
Then dip into powder and apply as usual.

Wear Your Jewelry Near Your Face

Wearing your sparkling earrings and necklaces by your face at night will make your face illuminate even more so in evening light.

Shine is Essential

Evening lighting calls for more shine and less powder. The problem is that you want your makeup to stay on and yet the powder can give off a "sallow" appearance in candle or evening light. If you really need the powder, always apply a touch of shine over the finished face.

Black Nights

When you're planning for candle lighting be aware that dressing in your favorite black dress will drain color from your face.
Compensate by intensifying color in the face and neck.
Alternatively choose a shiny dark color.

The Evening Bag

There is no way to look finished unless you have a great evening bag. Everyday bags will not segue into that special event. But you don't need to spend a lot of money on a bag that you will rarely use, and this is the perfect opportunity to show off your unique style.

Check the children's department. They have adorable versions of the most popular styles that will be just the right size for the perfect evening bag.

Take along one of those cute little bags that came with your jewelry.
Use a pretty cosmetic bag as an inexpensive chic clutch. Dress it up with a brooch.

Evening Bag Contents

Money and possibly a credit card
Lipstick and compact
Breath mints
Drivers license
Comb or folding brush

Optional

Cell phone
Mascara
Superglue to tack back false eyelashes

Body Prep

Avoid dairy on the day of a special event. It tends to make the body puffy.
Eliminate salt at least 24 hours before any special occasion.
Drink 8 to 10 glasses of water.
Cut out alcohol, which can bloat the body and face.
Stay away from carbonated beverages.

Decode That Invitation

The invitation came and you have no idea what to wear. Here are some general rules to follow so that you will look and feel appropriate.

Informal

Choose a classic look like a high end sweater with dressy pants or silk blouse with flowing silk pants. Finish off the look with classic heels and understated jewelry.

City Attire

A black trouser suit is always correct or choose a matching top and skirt or pants with two to three inch heels. A stacked heel is preferable over a stiletto.

Business/Cocktail

You can never go wrong with a basic black dress, always fashionable and chic. Add a jacket to tone it down until you feel comfortable in your surroundings. You can remove it later if warranted.

Formal

A long dress or skirt is called for, but you can get away with a mid calf skirt and highly embellished top. Compensate with elaborate jewelry if you don't have formal wear.

Black Tie

Even though this invitation implies a long dress, you can wear a dinner suit. Go for a formal but understated look..

Business Casual

Your every day business attire is perfectly acceptable as long as it is neat and chic. Add a few accessories and embellishments to bring it up to the notch of an occasion.

Chapter 18
Celebrity Beauty

Celebrities have tricks up their sleeve learned from everyone from their grandmas to their latest stylist. When they learn a trick that really works, they take it and add it to their regime.

Jessica Alba

Don't you love her lush lashes? There is an easy trick you can use to get the same results. Start with a lengthening and separating mascara. Coat lashes and let dry a moment. Then coat again, this time using a volumizing mascara. The two mascaras combined together produce incredible results!

To get to her fighting weight of 110 pounds, Jessica ate several small meals a day, did Pilates, some circuit training, and used the elliptical machine.

Scarlett Johansson

Known for her great pucker, Scarlett enhances her luscious lips by applying a dab of gloss on her lower lip which creates depth and shine. She also has a great trick for making her skin look dewy. Scarlett applies a small amount of moisturizer over her makeup to get a glow.

Rachel McAdams

This adorable beauty makes her green eyes pop by lining only the outer rims of the eye with a flat gray eye pencil. Gray is a color that can intensify any eye color. She keeps her healthy weight of 120 at 5'6" by adding a box of sprouts to her meals.

Christina Aguilera

The former fast food lover has dropped three dress sizes which she credits to a system known as sensory mix and match. She has one crunchy, one soft, one cold, and one hot food at every meal. Studies supporting this come from John Hopkins School of Medicine which claim that eating this way can dampen activity of orb frontal cortex neurons, cutting cravings by 30 per cent or more and keeping them suppressed for up to three hours.

Her stage look is often heavily made up. Christina relies on old fashioned pure petroleum jelly to remove it all.

Marcia Cross

Although this Desperate Housewife's favorite snack is Hot Tamales candy, her preferred exercise is speed walking which she alternates with regular yoga workouts.

Eva Longoria

A small spitfire on Desperate Housewives, Eva gets a wonderful glow on her face by using gold shimmer cream on her cheeks and forehead. Eva gets totally bored with constant exercise, but does like to work with large balance balls.

Oprah Winfrey

Finally past her widely talked about weight fluctuations, her tricks include keeping a journal of what she eats, drinking lots of water, and avoiding "white foods" including sugar, flour, and rice. Under her trainer Bob Green, Oprah tries to exercise daily combining cardio, weight bearing exercise, and stretching.

"I'm like every other woman: a closet full of clothes, but nothing to wear. So I just wear jeans." Cameron Diaz

Cameron looks great in her jeans weighing in at just 120 pounds on her 5'9" frame, and chooses sports over gyms.

Sela Ward

This 50 year old beauty attributes her looks to knowing what's right her at this time of her life. This includes longer hair, passing over trends for classic, tailored looks, and softer shades of makeup, and no more bright lipstick.

Sela allows herself a Krispy Kreme doughnut as a daily indulgence.

Rebecca Romijn

She keeps her weight at 135 by exercising with her fiancé, Jerry O'Connell. Rebecca loves (and does not deny herself) hamburgers, but instead of bread, has them wrapped in lettuce!

Lindsay Lohan

This talented actress and singer now weighs 118 and is committed to healthy ways of staying slim like free weights, cardio, and lots of sit ups. She drinks a cup of green tea every night to boost her metabolism. She also occasionally boxes with a trainer.

Christine Taylor

Married to Ben Stiller and the mother of two active pre schoolers, this comedic actress claims that running after her kids is what keeps her so thin. She also shares that she chooses fruit with cottage cheese as a meal every day.

Jennifer Aniston

Jen follows the Zone diet consisting of 40 percent carbs, 30 perfect fat and 30 percent protein. She runs and does yoga 3 times a week, uses an elliptical machine, and lifts 8 pound weights.

Known for her virtually flawless legs, Jennifer has her own cellulite treatment.
She wraps her legs in seaweed that she has first moistened with cod liver oil.
Jennifer also takes parsley tablets and includes it in her salads.

Her beauty trick for sparkling eyes is to apply taupe eye shadow over her lids, and then get them to "pop" by adding a small circle of gold shadow in the center of each eye.

Jennifer cleanses her skin with Neutrogena bar soap, which she has used since childhood. She claims that she is addicted to holistic face creams and masks.

Denise Richards uses Diet Designs, a home delivery service to help her stay in her size 26 jeans. She swims daily and chases after her children for exercise.

Heidi Klum maintains her figure with a breakfast of strawberries, a lunch of chicken and steamed spinach and veal and broccoli at dinner.
Heidi uses a hot oil treatment weekly on her processed hair to keep it soft and silky.

Halle Berry

When skin is as remarkable as Halle's, you know that it's the result of not only great genes, but great care. Halle has a nightly ritual of rubbing pure vitamin C on her face before she applies moisturizer.

Holly Robinson Peete

Thyme is Holly's secret. She grows it in her own garden, and boils it in a quart of water. She transfers it to a bowl, puts her face over the bowl with a towel over her head and steams her face.

Caprice

As a model and Surreal Life star, Caprice has a technique that many models use for keeping chlorine from discoloring her beautiful blonde hair. She rubs tomato ketchup into her hair after swimming. It prevents the green cast that can sometimes occur.

Star Jones

I so enjoyed working with Star when she co-hosted the View, and I can tell you that she enjoys and uses many of my beauty secrets. Her favorite is carrying baby wipes. Star uses it to remove makeup, cleanse her skin, and always chooses wipes with lanolin to add extra moisture to her skin.

Shannon Doherty

You'll never find powder in Shannon's makeup bag. She prefers a dewy, natural look and believes that the oil that shines through on her face makes her look youthful and fresh.

Terri Hatcher

A major feature on Terri's face is the look of finely arched eyebrows. She lines them with a soft powder, and then sets them by patting them down with hair spray.

Terri combines shimmer with liquid foundation to make her skin look dewy. She also mixes that shimmer with brown eye shadow powder to make her eyes stand out.

Drea DeMatteo

A strong magnifying mirror and tweezers are her best beauty allies. She claims that because of her ethnicity, she has to constantly keep her unruly brows neatly manicured.

Jennifer Garner

You won't find Jennifer spending a lot on her skin care. She uses cow udder cream to moisturize her face and body. She claims she copied this trick from Shania Twain.

Heather Locklear

Most celebrities will tell you that they drink tons of water. Heather drinks small sips throughout the day to stay hydrated. She finds that drinking large amounts of water leaves her feeling bloated. Not a big gym enthusiast, Heather prefers to play sports and only keeps wholesome foods in the house to encourage a healthy family atmosphere.

Heather is known for her gorgeous hair. Her conditioner of choice is a combination of eggs and olive oil, used as a pre shampoo treatment. Take one egg and combine with two tablespoons of extra virgin olive oil. Apply to dry hair and leave on for 30 minutes. Shampoo and condition.

Pink

The singer use sugar to keep her skin glowing. Pink uses a very gentle facial cleanser, then dips her fingers into a bowl of sugar which she uses as an over all exfoliant.

Gwyneth Paltrow

Talk about a star babying her skin! Gwyneth uses Johnson's Baby Lotion to keep her skin smooth. She adores the scent! She is careful with everything she eats, and when not pregnant fills up on swordfish.

Angelina Jolie

Although Angelina admits she used to have some not great eating habits in the past, she's now totally reformed. Her favorite beverage is soy milk, and she prefers steamed vegetables. Angelina's favorite snack which she keeps by her side is breakfast cereal.

Pamela Anderson

An ardent animal lover and PETA spokesperson, Pamela is a strict vegetarian.
She will not eat meat, chicken, or seafood. When hunger strikes, sugar free gum is her ally.

Madonna

Although occasionally Madonna enjoys an ale with her husband, she stays true to a macrobiotic diet which consists of whole grains, beans, vegetables, some meats, and fish.
She reveals that her best skin secret also provides her with energy. Madonna's flawless complexion is invigorated by oxygen facials. She uses them to combat fatigue and jet lag.
Madonna's favorite makeup trick is using burgundy mascara to emphasize her eyes.

Julia Roberts

This mega star admits to a bad habit of biting her nails and cuticle area. It's why she keeps her nails short. To soften her hands she soaks her nails in warm olive oil.
Julia prefers a natural look and applies a tinted moisturizer as a base.

Kate Moss

This reformed model carries lavender to help her relax. She not only sniffs it throughout the day, but keeps a sachet in her pillow to help her sleep.

Jennifer Lopez

This Latina actress/singer has the softest skin in the business, and to keep it that way she stocks up on cocoa butter lotion. Her absolutely essential beauty secret is to get at least nine to ten hours of sleep a night.

Garcelle Beavais

Aloe Vera gel is a great humectant. This actress stores it in the refrigerator, and spreads it all over her face before applying her moisturizer.
When she wants to drop a few pounds Garcelle drinks water mixed with lemon and cayenne pepper.

Lucy Liu

The Charlie's Angel applies equal parts of cornmeal and water. She creates a soft paste which she applies all over her body as a gentle, yet effective exfoliant.

Lucy eats a large lunch and small dinner. It's the old "breakfast like a king, lunch like a prince, dinner like a pauper" rule that many celebrities use to keep their weight down.

Catherine Zeta Jones

A star, who embraces, doesn't hide behind her curves. She refuses to crash diet after seeing so many eating disorders from her dancing years. Besides dancing, her exercise of choice is golf. Her other beauty secrets include soaking her hands in water and denture tablets for whiter nails, and mixing up glycerin and sea salt and rubbing it all over her body. Catherine admits although it "stinks to high heaven" she pours beer on her hair for great shine.

Queen Latifah

The "Queen" shares a wonderful tip that she inherited from her beloved grandmother who taught her to use baking soda as an exfoliant.

Jane Seymour

The ageless actress hates going out for her treatments. She prefers to do everything from head to toe in the privacy of her home, and she's constantly experimenting on herself.

Kate Winslet

How did Kate lose 50 pounds after giving birth? She sliced up a large cucumber each day and kept it on her kitchen counter. It was the perfect low calorie hunger stopper with a mere 28 calories for a medium cucumber.

Gisele Bundchen

The Brazilian super model eats spicy foods and douses just about all her food with hot sauce. It raises the metabolism by creating a thermogenic burn.

Nicole Kidman

Every star watches her weight and Nicole is no exception. She snacks on raisins.
She dips them in honey and arranges them on celery. She calls it "frogs on a log".
Her secret to looking fresh-faced is to meticulously match her brows to her current hair color.

Jennifer Love Hewitt

A highly defined food program is the source of Jennifer's fabulous body.
The actress splits up her food and eats each separately. She eats her vegetables before her meat.
Jennifer believes that her body digests food better this way.
When it comes to beauty, Jennifer uses pink lip gloss as a long lasting blush to keep her face
dewy and fresh all day.

Kim Cattrall

You've seen her body from every angle during her stint on Sex in the City, and surely want to
know how she kept herself in such tremendous shape. Walking throughout New York at a
super fast pace was one way, and the other, lemon juice. She squeezes it on her salads,
vegetables, fish, and even on French fries. It is known to suppress the appetite, flavor food
without the calories, and help dissolve fat.

Reese Witherspoon

Is there stress after winning an Oscar? If so, Reese knows how to get rid of it. Stress can wreak
havoc on your looks. She duct tapes two tennis balls together, then stretches out on a mat, and
rolls up and down on the balls which are positioned on each side of her spine.

Mariah Carey

Would you believe that this singing diva has a secret from the baking aisle of her local grocery
store? Mariah adds a drop or two of peppermint extract to her lip gloss to give her lips a pouty
look. The mint increases blood flow to the lip. If you have skin sensitivity test it on your wrist
before applying it to your lips.
Mariah has lost over 30 pounds, going from 170 pounds to 138. At 5'9" she credits her success

to what she calls the "morsel diet". This is her own approach to mini meals that she spreads throughout the day. She lets herself have everything she wants, but only allows herself a forkful serving. Although she worked with a trainer for an hour a day, her favorite way to work out is in water. She stands shoulder deep in a pool and runs.

Claudia Schiffer

Still fabulously fit, Claudia attributes her ability to maintain her weight by eating lots of fruit. In fact, that's all she eats until noon. Even her best beauty secret is sweet. She uses Cherry Jell-O as a long lasting lip stain. Just dip a dampened cotton swab into the Jell-O and swipe it all over the lip area. Smudge it with a coat of lip gloss.

Anna Nicole

Part of her success with successfully losing 70 pounds is dieting of course, but she also attributes it with taking a colon cleansing laxative on a "regular" basis. It not only accelerated her weight loss but Anna claims it detoxified her body.

Maria Menounos

The Access Hollywood correspondent lost 20 pounds in 5 months by cutting her portions in half without cutting out any of her favorite foods. She went from eating six slices of pizza in a sitting to two.

Sharon Stone

At 48 years old, Sharon has the most incredible abs. She credits her six pack to a jackknives routine she learned from a tightrope walker in Africa. She does 10 to 15 daily. You won't find Sharon at the gym. She uses her every day activities to keep her youthful body by doing such things as parking her car away from her destination, running up the stairs, and never taking elevators or escalators. She goes for ten minute bursts of energy.

Emily Rossum

The beautiful star of Phantom of the Opera and Poseidon has a unique philosophy. She only eats foods that look as close as possible to the way they were in nature.

Penelope Cruz

This curvy spitfire doesn't ever work out. In fact she has stated that she finds it very boring to have to be skinny all the time. To ease her sweet tooth, she treats herself to diet Popsicles. At only 15 calories each, she allows herself up to eight a day.

Cher

Here's a great trick from a mega diva. Cher rubs a damp eyebrow brush on a bar of glycerin soap then combs her brows into shape. The soap dries quickly without making the brows look lacquered

Hilary Swank

Although greatly geared down from her arduous workouts for Million Dollar Baby, Hilary has maintained a lean muscular body by eating lots of protein and high fiber vegetables. Her favorite vegetables are cabbage, kale, and asparagus.

Kelly Osbourne

Having overcome her self esteem issues and slimming down to a healthy 126 at 5'2", Kelly has her own winners.
She has learned to love healthy foods, and to substitute grapes, raisins, and apple slices for processed foods and chocolate.

Sandra Bernhardt

When this talented comedian was struggling she decided to try manicuring. She sears that the secret of a great pedicure is putting Sea Breeze in the water. It cools and deodorizes the foot.

Salma Hayek

This is a great tip that will help other beauties who have both dark hair and dark eyebrows. Since Salma's skin is porcelain beige, her dark eyebrows overwhelm her face. When her eyebrows can't be bleached, gold eye shadow or gold mascara do the trick to lighten them

Jessica Simpson

Keeping her "Dukes of Hazard" figure hasn't been easy for Jessica. Lifting weights three times a week has helped, as well as staying away from salty snacks, sugar and her beloved southern cooking.

Janet Jackson

With constant weight fluctuations, it's not an easy job for Janet to keep a low weight. What has helped is eating five times a day to keep her metabolism fired up. She has successfully lost 60 pounds, going from 180 pounds to 120.

Sarah Jessica Parker

Known for her lithe yet compact figure, she maintains it by eating two or three egg whites with cheese for breakfast, one can of tuna with mayonnaise for lunch, and tuna sushi for dinner. By now you must know that she loves tuna!

Nicole Richie

The Simple Life star and shockingly thin tabloid subject claims she loses her appetite when stressed. The reason she can't eat is admittedly psychological. She claims she feels like something is "eating her up" inside.

Sheryl Crow

This singer weighs just 105 pounds and keeps it there by eating a hearty breakfast which sometimes includes a Mexican burrito with cheese, salsa, and sausage. Her exercise routine is either running or biking for an hour each day. She has given up caffeine, and takes a fish oil supplement daily.

Uma Thurman

It's hard to believe, but this beautiful towering actress loves sweets. In fact, she loves them so much that she eats breakfast and lunch only! Her evening meal consists of one of her favorite chocolate concoctions.

Timeless Celebrities

Sophia Loren

This 70+ Italian beauty has used olive oil on her face and body all her life. She warms it up and uses it on her hair as a pre conditioner, and rough spots on her hands, feet, and knees. Sophia loves her pasta, but only a cup at a time.

Candice Bergen

The Boston Legal classic beauty swears she looks younger when she is wearing less makeup. Her favorite face is a little bit of powder on imperfections, a bright lipstick, and curl enhancing mascara.

Rene Russo

This model turned actress had to spend four years of her life in a body cast to correct scoliosis. The experience has led her to maintain her youthful figure by using the Feldenkrais method, an exercise program that improves posture while alleviating pain.

Elizabeth Hurley

Watercress soup is the "go to" weight loss tool when this British beauty has to lose a few pounds. She used it to lose her pregnancy weight and still relies on it when she is making an appearance to sell her own bathing suit line.

Reba McEntire

Rodeo star turned singer turned actress Reba is a curvy 5'6" and 125 pounds. She weighed in at 140 in college because of college beer parties. Although she no longer imbibes in beer, she does "juice" twice a day and drinks water every two hours.

Chapter 19
Insider Travel

Traveling well is a best kept secret of insiders. It makes all the difference in how comfortable you will be while traveling, and how you will enjoy your final destination. There's no reason to let your looks go when you do.

Packing Tips

Luggage
Choose luggage that is both light and durable. Modern materials are now available that weights almost nothing and performs like their heavier counterparts. Also avoid luggage that has no bend or give to it.

Divide and Conquer
Separate your bag into two sections.

On the bottom of your bag pack your heavy items like shoes and bagged cosmetics. This is key to preventing your bag from toppling over.

Stuff your shoes with your jewelry.

Button and zipper everything to fight wrinkling.

In the top section of your bag, lay your jackets, dresses, skirts, and pants.

Insert your shirts, underwear, swimsuit, and lighter items.

Fold your heavy items over these items to secure them.

Pack as tightly as possible. Loose clothing wrinkles more easily.

Pack stretch cotton and knits for minimum care and wrinkling.

Choose the same color scheme for easy mixing and matching that will stretch your travel wardrobe.

Place shoes in ripped hose or plastic bags.

Choose items that can be layered, so you can adapt and be comfortable if the weather should change.

Pack a stain remover so that a mishap can be cleaned quickly, and you won't have to leave the item aside for the rest of your trip.

Packing Trick

When packing necklaces, run them through a straw and clasp. This prevents knots and tangles.

Double Up

Use shampoo as a body wash and also to wash fine fabrics.
Body lotion doubles as a leave-in hair conditioner.

Avoid Packing

Linen
Jeans (if you need to bring them, wear them)
Hair dryers & irons (all hotels have them in the room or at your request)
Heavy shoes or boots

Insider Tip

Duct tape is a lifesaver when traveling. Take about a foot of it, and wrap it around a pen or pencil.
Use it for emergencies like purse handle breaks, shoe separations, and for emergency suitcase closing.

Look Good While Flying

Don't fall into the trap of wearing a sweats or a jogging suit. You'll never get upgraded to first class if you do, and you'll "shout" tourist all the way.
Allow for temperature changes by wearing layers which can be removed easily.
Go light on your makeup. The air in the cabin has an unforgiving way of clogging pores and creating other havoc with your skin.
Bring a shawl or pashmina to drape or to use as a pillow.
Insiders always carry a travel kit which may include ear plugs, their own headphones, neck pillow, and wipes for teeth.

While in the Air

Drink plenty of water to counter act the drying effect of "canned" air.

Wear glasses instead of contact lenses.

Bring slippers or slipper socks to keep your feet warm when you slip off your shoes.

Security Alert

Make sure you have all prescriptions in your name so that you are allowed to travel with them. Check your purse for gel or liquid cosmetics and leave them at home. You would hate to have them confiscated.

Purse Must

Pack facial tissues at all times in case you come across a restroom that doesn't have toilet paper. Never carry a purse that looks like your life is in it. If traveling for business fit a purse inside your briefcase.

Stay Fit on the Road

Pack a jump rope and resistance band. They don't take up much space and will become invaluable for a quick workout.

If you're short on packing space, consider trading in pajamas for workout wear in your suitcase.

Take advantage of your gym membership if you belong to a chain. Many gyms have a passport program that allows you to work out at many different clubs.

Join a club for a day. Ask your hotel if they have a health club that they maintain a relationship with. Many without their own facilities offer this amenity.

Walk through the airport before your flight and during layovers. Some airports now offer gyms, spas, and fitness centers for travelers.

While in your seat, push your heels into the floor and contract your buttocks for in your seat firming.

While in your hotel utilize the large telephone books to do step ups.

Favorite Space Savers

Cleansing cloths
Moisturizers with sunscreen
Film canisters to store jewelry and other small items.
Crystal or rhinestone jewelry to turn casual clothing into party time!
By all means keep the real stuff at home!

Insider Tip

Forget the nail polish and have your nails buffed to save both space and maintenance while traveling.

Traveling Essentials

Always be sure to pack a little black dress (preferably in a knit) to wear from day to evening.

Carry or pack a sweater that can keep you warm or dress up an outfit. A jacket is just too heavy to pack.

Shoe Concerns

Wear mules while flying so that you can get back into your shoes when you've landed. Your feet will swell considerably while in the air and you may not be able to get back into them.

Plan Ahead

Pack plastic supermarket bags to hold wet and dirty items.
Take along a foldable bag for souvenirs.
Measure your carry on luggage. While the accepted maximum height for on board luggage is 22 inches, each airline has its own size restrictions.
Label your luggage both inside and out. The tag could come off in transit.
Include your destination address and phone number.

Safety on the Road

Choose hotels with interior room entrances.
Avoid hotels with hallways that lead to a parking lot, garage, or maintenance area.

Ask for a room close to the elevator.

Use the Do Not Disturb sign even while you're out of your room.

Never accept a first floor room. Always request a higher floor.

A smaller hotel and lobby are safer than a large hotel since the their staff are trained to notice strangers and loiterers.

Keep an identification tag on you if you have any medical precautions.

Drink bottled water whenever you can.

Keep a small first aid kit nearby.

Model Travel

When a model travels to a warm climate, you can bet she is carrying at least three bathing suits so that she can ensure that she has one to wear while the other two are drying.

A rubber spatula may seem like an odd travel companion, but it's a must for models. A rubber spatula comes in handy from everything to popping a can of diet soda without breaking a nail to performing the duty of an extra wide shoe horn.

A scarf is the preferred mode of transport for carrying cosmetic brushes They will not crush, stay sanitary, and remain in perfect condition.

Chapter 20
Finishing Touches

Accessories are a great way to show off your personality and style, and turn basic clothing into special statements. Here are my guidelines on every insider's favorite finishing touch, jewelry.

1. The more basic your outfit, the more jewelry you can wear.
2. If your jewelry doesn't feel totally comfortable and effortless then you have too much on.
3. Jewelry should never overcome the look.
4. Your accessories should never wear you, you are the star.
5. Always group the same type of jewelry together.

Insiders Tip
Always give yourself a final check in front of a full length mirror. If your eye goes right to the piece you are wearing, take it off.

Earrings
If earrings are more than one inch in length, you should always skip the pendant.

Bracelets
Wear more than one on your wrist, but employ a color or theme for the chicest look.
Pair a couple with your watch. Coordinate design or colors.

Wrap a necklace around your wrist several times to create a "multi strand" look.

Pearls
Always a classic, update your pearls by adding a pendant for a less traditional look.

Jewelry Sensitivity
If your earrings, necklace, or bracelet leave your ea lobes and skin itchy and red, you may have an allergy to nickel. It's a metal used to add strength to jewelry and can cause swelling and a rash.

Remedies

1. Coat jewelry with clear nail polish.
2. Treat your skin with Evening Primrose Oil. It acts like a natural topical steroid at relieving skin itching and redness. Use it regularly, especially when wearing nickel filled jewelry.

Scarves

A scarf is a fabulous accessory and can be worn in so many different ways.
They can be intimidating and if worn too carefully can look overly ostentatious.
Scarves are a styling finishing touch in cashmere or "faux" materials and can be worn to give extra panache as a topping to a warm coat. Scarves extend their style when matched to gloves. Fur lined gloves are warmest in leather or faux leather.

Neck Wrap

Fold a rectangular scarf lengthwise. Wrap it around your neck, bringing the scarf ends to the front of the neck. Open the loop, and pull the loose ends through the folded loop.
Tighten the ends until the scarf fits comfortably.

Shoulder Drape

For this look use a large square scarf. Fold it into a triangle, and place that triangle over one shoulder. Knot it at, or slightly in front of the opposite shoulder.

Head Wrap

To keep scarves from looking contrived, or that you just tried too hard to get dressed today, you need to use your scarf casually. Your scarf should always be an after thought.
The French know how to wear scarves this way. They will tie it to a purse to coordinate with their outfit, or throw it over a shoulder just because they might need it later. That's the look you're going for.

Fold a rectangular scarf two times over so that the width is about two inches wide.
Place the scarf to the front of the head like a headband, and then tie the ends slightly to one side so that the hanging ends are still visible.

Handbags

I believe that handbags are THE most important finishing touch. After all, you carry a handbag right at eye level. You are constantly pulling it out for purchases, touching up, showing identification, etc. Insiders no longer match their shoes and their bags. Quite the opposite, many choose a bag in a big bright color to be even more noticed. There are some guidelines to follow so that you'll love your bag will remain your favorite finishing touch.

1. Be sure to pick up the bag before purchasing it. Make sure it's nice and light before your items go inside. If possible, place your wallet and a few other of your regular items into the bag you plan on purchasing to be sure that everything fits and can be moved in and out conveniently.
2. Wear your bag where you body is slimmest. For instance, if you're top heavy, it won't flatter your body to have a short shoulder strap. You'll look top heavy. You can actually balance out your body with the right bag.

Belts

Wear them in interesting ways to make them modern and to create your signature.
A long beaded necklace looks great around the waist if it is long enough.
Wearing a belt in the same shade as your skirt or pant is most slimming.

Shoes

Purchase shoes at the end of the day when your feet are swollen.
Choose higher heels one half to one full size larger than your normal shoe size.
Shoes should be flexible and bend naturally where the foot is widest.
Toes should have room to wiggle in the toe box.
Shoes should be light weight when lifted.
Check to see the way your heels stand. If it falls over on the shelf, then they are simply not stable and you'll probably fall over too.

Insider Tip

Choose synthetic socks. Cotton just doesn't keep your feet dry.

Glasses

For some women glasses are an every day necessity. For others, they're for reading, or for taking a break from contact lenses. Glasses are a great way to accentuate your beauty and style, but done incorrectly can detract from your looks.

Foundation can tend to rub off on glasses. To avoid this press powder on the inner eye and anywhere else where your glasses will rub.

When you wear glasses it's important to emphasize your brows. A bolder brow will bring the emphasis to your brow, and not to your glasses.

If your glasses minimize your eyes, always line your eyes to make them stand out. Be sure to curl your lashes to awaken them under your glasses and to prevent them from hitting the lens.

With glasses that make your eyes stand out, be careful with your makeup. Make sure that your mascara doesn't clump and that you don't overdo the shadow.

Frame Style

Never purchase frames that are too heavy. There are great styles in lightweight plastics.

If you have a long narrow face, you'll look best in wrap around or oval frames.
A round face should look for square glasses.
A square face is flattered by round glasses.

If your glasses minimize your eyes, always line your eyes to make them stand out, and curl your lashes to awaken them under your glasses.

Although tinted lenses are never styling, do look for shades with UV protection of at least 95 per cent blockage. Polarized lenses will cut glare.

More Eyewear Styling

If your glasses are colored, that's all the color you need on your eyes. Make up shades should be neutral. Coordinate or match the color of your glasses to your lips.

Choose frames in a shade that you would select a beautiful sweater, a color that always gets you compliments

Chapter 21
Beauty Recipes

Ginger Scrub

This scrub will boost circulation and make skin glow!

2 cups brown sugar
1 cup honey
2 teaspoons ground ginger
3 teaspoons lemon juice

Combine ingredients and rub all over body before showering.
Rub off with a coarse washcloth, loofah, or vegetable brush, using circular motions.

Grapefruit Foot Scrub

You'll love how the grapefruit's citric acid and antioxidants help turn over new skin cells while softening hardened skin.

Juice of 1 Grapefruit
1 cup sugar
1 cup sea salt

Mix ingredients together in a bowl.
Massage into feet.

Rinse thoroughly and pat dry.

Chamomile & Milk Bath Relaxer

Chamomile has the ability to calm and soothe.
Milk is a softener and an exfoliant.
At the end of the day treat yourself to this relaxing bath that will leave you rested, and with soft
smooth skin.

Steep 5 chamomile tea bags in 1 cup boiling water
Brew for at least 20 minutes.
Add tea to 2 quarts hot milk
Pour into running bath water and swirl.

Soak until the water cools.

Rosemary Hair Treatment

Rosemary benefits hair by removing product build up.
The aroma of rosemary will energize your spirits and your scalp.

½ cup dried rosemary
½ cup olive oil

Sprinkle the rosemary into the olive oil.
Microwave mixture until warm but not hot.
Massage into hair and scalp.
Wrap hair in warm towel
Hint: Heat towel in dryer.

Leave mixture in for at least twenty minutes.
Shampoo out thoroughly.

Seaweed Face Mask

This is a face mask that will draw bloat from the face while firming.

½ cup dried or powdered seaweed (available at health food stores)
1 tablespoon warm water

Stir together in a small bowl until a thick paste forms.

Spread over face with a pastry brush.
Allow to dry.
Rinse thoroughly with cool water.
Follow up with a moisturizer.

Cucumber Lemon Whitener

Use this treatment to lighten dark, rough areas of the body.

Juice of one lemon
A teaspoon of turmeric (available in the baking aisle)

Mix both together until you create a soft paste.
Apply with an old clean toothbrush to darkened elbows, under arms, and neck.
Rub in steadily in a circular motion.
Allow to set and penetrate for about ten minutes.
Rinse with warm water.
Pat thoroughly dry.

Orange Yogurt Mask

Use this refreshing mask to thoroughly cleanse while nourishing skin.

1 teaspoon plain yogurt
Juice of half of a small orange

Combine ingredients and smooth all over face and neck with fingertips.
Leave on to set for about 10 to 15 minutes.
Rinse with tepid water.
Allow skin to air dry.

Blueberry Toner

This wonderfully refreshing face toner is offered at a top spa for $85.00!

3 teaspoons blueberries
¼ cup plain yogurt

Microwave blueberries in a safe container for 10 seconds.
Add yogurt, and whip with a fork until the mixture is frothy.

Apply mixture to face and neck.
Allow to penetrate at least 10 minutes.
Rinse off with cool water.

Ultimate Pore Cleanser

This is an at home version of the popular "strips" that are being sold to remove blackheads and clogged pores.

1 teaspoon unflavored gelatin
1 1/2 teaspoons milk

Mix above together in a small microwave safe bowl.
Microwave for 5 to 7 seconds.
Test to feel that the mixture is warm but not hot.
Apply to nose and chin area with a small pastry brush.
Allow it to dry.
It should take about 10 minutes, and you should be left with a stiff film.
Gently peel off.

This cleanser takes practice.
Make sure to apply enough of the paste to create a solid film.

Hair Mask

This easy to make hair treatment will give your hair incredible shine and bounce while sealing split ends. It will save you lots of money, and is a cinch to make. You'll love this recipe!

2 tablespoons olive oil
2 tablespoons honey
1 egg yolk

Combine above ingredients and heat in microwave until warm (about 10 seconds)
Massage into hair, concentrating on ends.
Wrap hair in a towel or shower cap.
Leave on for about 30 minutes.
Rinse out thoroughly with warm water.
Shampoo & condition.

Foot Fetish

Here is a relaxing foot treatment that will leave your hard working tootsies soft, invigorated, and smelling great!

1 cup lemon juice
2 teaspoons ground cinnamon
2 tablespoons olive oil
1/2 cup milk

Heat above ingredients in the microwave until just warm to the touch.
Soak feet until the liquid becomes cool.
Finish by brushing feet vigorously with a vegetable brush.
Rinse and pat feet dry.

Final Thoughts

It has been my intent in writing this book to not only give you a glimpse into the world of beauty, diet, and fashion, but also to allow you access to the very techniques and tricks used behind the scenes.

I have laid these tips out in a way to make them practical and easy to include into your daily regimes.

Take away what will work for you, and use this book as a reference when you face your own beauty dilemma or need to think things through. Feel free to glean and polish and rework these ideas to make them your own.

Beauty is universal yet highly personal. There are many options today, and it is my greatest wish that you experiment, have some fun, and then go on and live your life beautifully and with your own indelible insignia.

About the Author

Diane Irons started as a model at the age of 13 and then went on to become an award winning journalist, syndicated talk show host, and best selling author. Her passion is beauty and the right of every woman to look and feel her best. She has dedicated her life's work to sharing all she learns with her world wide audience. Diane has worked with countless celebrities in the entertainment and fashion industries.

Her expertise has been sought by Good Morning America, the View, CNN, E Entertainment, 700 Club, Fox News, CBS, Inside Edition, Lifetime, and Entertainment Tonight.

Diane has been featured in the Wall Street Journal, Redbook, Cosmopolitan, Woman's World, Ladies Home Journal, Allure, First for Women, Star, the Globe, and the Enquirer.

More information is available at
DianeIrons.com

Contact Diane at dianeirons@aol.com

Index

NOTES

NOTES

NOTES

NOTES

NOTES

NOTES

NOTES